WORD DETECTIVE

130 GAMES AND PUZZLES
TO IMPROVE SPELLING

GRADE 2

Ann Richmond Fisher

Illustrations by Joel and Ashley Selby

**ROCKRIDGE
PRESS**

Interior and Cover Designer: Brian Lewis

Art Producer: Karen Beard

Editor: Justin Hartung

Production Manager: Oriana Siska

Production Editor: Melissa Edeburn

Illustrations ©2019 Joel and Ashley Selby

ISBN: Print 978-1-64152-960-0

CONTENTS

INTRODUCTION

I love words, including word games, word puzzles, word lists, and spelling words! Some of my friends and relatives collect teacups, books, nativity sets, and postcards. I collect WORDS!

During my time as a classroom teacher, I wrote word games to add variety to spelling and English lessons. Word puzzles, as you may already know, are wonderful tools for teaching spelling skills and enhancing students' vocabularies.

That's why it's been so much fun to write this book. I've compiled a targeted list of 200 second-grade spelling words and plugged them into 130 engaging games and puzzles.

This book also includes a fun mystery for children to solve. First, they'll read "The Case of the Hidden Gold." Then, as they solve the puzzles, they will uncover secret letters to help crack the case. When all the puzzles have been solved, your young detective will be able to spell the answer to the mystery.

NOTE: When your child finishes the book, visit CallistoMediaBooks.com/WordDetective2 to get 20 free bonus puzzles.

HOW TO USE THIS BOOK

Your word detective is about to set off on a spelling and sleuthing adventure!

As your second grader works through this book, he or she will practice 200 words. The words are arranged in 10 chapters by theme, including family, friends, and animals. In each chapter, the first 10 words tend to be slightly easier than the second set of words. Students are likely to encounter most of these words in their world.

Students will practice these words by completing lots of fun puzzles. As a parent or teacher, you should be sure the student understands the directions for each puzzle before beginning to solve it.

With your student, spend some time reading and discussing "The Case of the Hidden Gold" on page vi before beginning the activities. Tell your student that he or she will be the word detective who will solve this mystery. As your student completes the puzzles in this book, he or she will find special letters under a magnifying glass, which should be written in order in the back of this book on page 166.

When all the puzzles are solved, the letters will reveal the location of the hidden gold, and your student will receive a special Word Detective badge. Now turn the page to start cracking the case!

THE CASE OF THE HIDDEN GOLD

"Grandma, we're here!" called Jane and Karl. "We came over right away. Why do you need our help?" they asked. Franklin, Grandma's furry dog, wagged his tail and barked.

"I found a very old note from my grandfather. It says he hid three gold coins on my farm, and he wanted me to find them someday. I don't know where I should start looking," Grandma said.

Jane and Karl loved Grandma's farm. They liked to eat the peas and beans from her garden. They liked the apples from her apple trees. They liked to walk around the pond and explore the woods. But besides Grandma, Franklin was the best part about coming to Grandma's farm.

Grandma loved Franklin, too. She built a fancy doghouse for him. She cut out windows for him and hung little red curtains. She gave him a fan when the temperature was too hot outside. She gave him blankets when the weather was cold.

Jane said, "Let's start looking for the gold. Why don't we look under your apple trees?" The three walked around every tree, looking for something shiny. But they didn't see anything.

Karl thought they should walk around the pond to look for a hiding spot. They did, but they had no luck.

Grandma said, "We're never going to find the gold this way. My grandfather hid the coins when I was only four years old. They could be very deep in the ground by now. Or maybe someone else already found them."

Franklin rubbed against Grandma's leg trying to make her feel better.

"Franklin is such a good friend," said Grandma. "If only he could talk, he could help us find the gold."

What Grandma didn't know is that Franklin has a secret. He's not just a dog—he's a detective! He wants to find the gold, but he needs your help.

As you solve the puzzles in this book, you will see special letters under a magnifying glass. When you find a letter, write it in the back of this book on page 166. When you finish all the puzzles, you'll find out where the gold is hidden!

Let's get started, word detectives . . .

CHAPTER
ONE

- - - - - -

Family

Words to Learn

Write each word in the blank.

1. mother   _____

2. father   _____

3. sister   _____

4. brother   _____

5. baby   _____

6. uncle   _____

7. aunt   _____

8. pets   _____

9. home   _____

10. family   _____

Write your hardest words again here:

_____

_____

_____

Merry-Go-Round

Start at any letter and move around the circle, either forward or backward, to find one of your spelling words. Circle the first letter. Write the word under each circle.

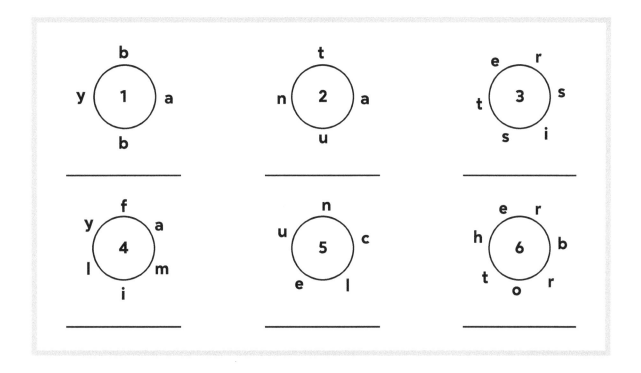

Letter Slides

Slide letters from the first word down to the second using the arrow. Keep going, sliding letters from each word down to the word below it, until you have reached the end of each slide.

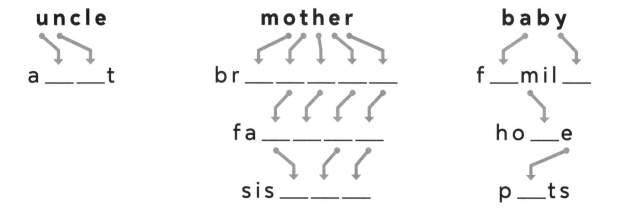

uncle

a ___ ___ ___ t

mother

br ___ ___ ___ ___ ___ ___

fa ___ ___ ___ ___ ___

sis ___ ___ ___ ___

baby

f ___ mil ___

ho ___ e

p ___ ts

Write a sentence using one of these words.

_____

_____

Box Stop

Write one word from the box in each blank. You will not use all the words.

aunt	home	family	baby	pets
father	sister	brother	mother	uncle

1. My dad is also called my _____

2. My mom is also called my _____

3. My mother's brother is my _____

4. My uncle's wife is my _____

5. A girl who has the same parents as me is my _____

6. A boy who has the same parents as me is my _____

7. The place where I live is my _____

8. My animals are my _____

Places, Please

Add each of your spelling words to this puzzle. Use the letters shown to help you.
Cross off each word after you put it in the puzzle. Write your word again in the blank.

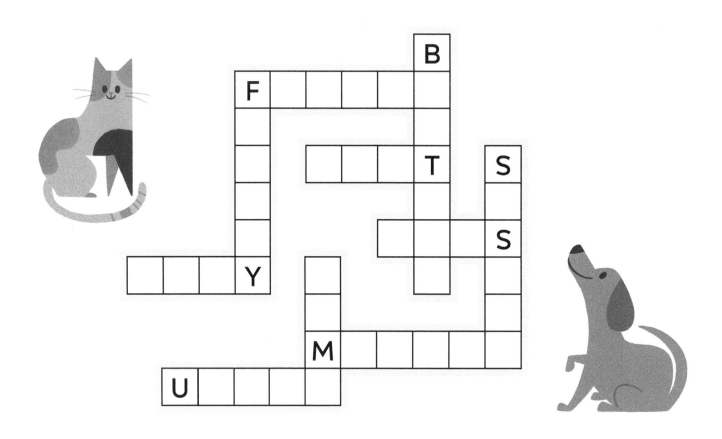

uncle _____

aunt _____

pets _____

home _____

family _____

baby _____

sister _____

brother _____

mother _____

father _____

Crack the Code

Use the code provided to find your spelling words. Write each letter as you solve it. For example, 5 3 8 would be pet.

1. ? & 9 8

    ___ ___ ___ ___

2. * + 8 6 3 2

    ___ ___ ___ ___ ___ ___

3. # ? * $ 4 1

    ___ ___ ___ ___ ___ ___

4. & 9 7 4 3

    ___ ___ ___ ___ ___

5. 6 + * 3

    ___ ___ ___ ___

6. ! $! 8 3 2

    ___ ___ ___ ___ ___ ___

1 = y	! = s
2 = r	# = f
3 = e	* = m
4 = l	+ = o
5 = p	$ = i
6 = h	& = u
7 = c	? = a
8 = t	
9 = n	

Be Choosy!

Choose the best answer and circle it. Write the word in the blank.

1. Sometimes I visit my aunt and _____.

   home   pets   uncle

2. When my _____ brother was born, I helped take care of him.

   sister   baby   father

3. Because my _____ is a pilot, he does not come home every night.

   father   mother   sister

4. After school I give my _____ fresh food and water.

   family   pets   home

5. I asked my _____ if she would play ball with me.

   sister   baby   brother

Words to Learn

Write each word in the blank.

1. child   _____

2. parent   _____

3. grandpa _____

4. grandma _____

5. love   _____

6. trust   _____

7. sharing   _____

8. caring   _____

9. helpful   _____

10. together _____

Write your hardest words again here:

_____

_____

_____

Tic-Tac-Toe

Circle every word spelled correctly. Draw a line across three of them to score a tic-tac-toe. Write the misspelled words correctly on the lines below.

granpa	careing	parent
togther	helpful	love
grandma	trust	shareing

_____

_____

_____

Word Search

Circle each word you find in the word search. Words may go up, down, or across, both backward and forward. Write each word as you find it.

l	g	u	a	r	d	l	i	h	c
o	g	r	a	n	d	m	a	r	e
v	j	p	g	p	j	s	t	k	f
e	j	a	r	m	h	h	o	e	g
u	c	r	a	z	e	a	g	x	t
b	a	e	n	y	l	r	e	z	r
q	r	n	d	c	p	i	t	e	u
k	i	t	p	e	f	n	h	c	s
h	n	u	a	z	u	g	e	z	t
l	g	z	h	q	l	n	r	l	a

grandpa _____

grandma _____

parent _____

child _____

helpful _____

together _____

caring _____

sharing _____

love _____

trust _____

Be Choosy!

Choose the best answer and circle it. Write the word in the blank.

1. It's fun to work _____ as a family.

   trust   love   together

2. My father is a _____.

   parent   helpful   grandma

3. Your mother's mother is your _____.

   grandpa   grandma   child

4. I _____ to spend time with family.

   trust   love   caring

5. My sister and I like _____ treats from our grandma.

   caring   sharing   trust

Letter Slides

Slide one letter from the first word down to the second using the arrow. Keep going, sliding letters from each word down to the word below it, until you have reached the end of each slide.

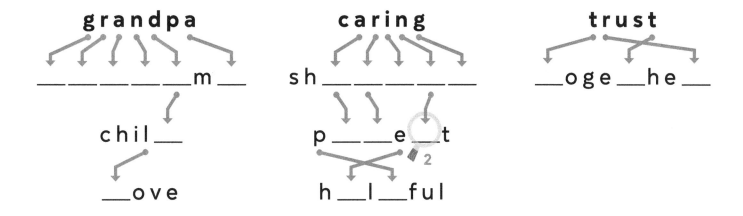

grandpa

__ __ __ __ __ __ m __

chil __

__ o v e

caring

s h __ __ __ __ __ __

p __ __ e __ t
2

h __ l __ f u l

trust

__ o g e __ h e __

Write a sentence using one of these words.

_____

_____

Remember to add letters in the magnifying glasses
to page 166 to solve the mystery!

Crack the Code

Use the code provided to find your spelling words. Write each letter as you solve it.

1. 6 8 ! # 6

    —— —— —— —— ——

2. # 4 2 8 ^ 3 7

    —— —— —— —— —— —— ——

3. 9 1 + 5

    —— —— —— ——

4. 7 8 2 3 ? & 2

    —— —— —— —— —— —— ——

5. & 2 8 5 3 6

    —— —— —— —— —— ——

6. 7 8 2 3 ? * 2

    —— —— —— —— —— —— ——

1 = o	* = m
2 = a	+ = v
3 = n	? = d
4 = h	! = u
5 = e	# = s
6 = t	^ = i
7 = g	& = p
8 = r	
9 = l	

Missing Letters

Add the missing letters to finish the spelling words.

1.   h ___ ___ e

2.   t r ___ ___ ___

3.   ___ h a ___ i ___ g

4.   c ___ i ___ ___

5.   p a ___ ___ ___ t

6.   c a ___ ___ ___ g

7.   h e ___ ___ ___ u ___

8.   t ___ ___ e t ___ ___ r

Write a sentence using one of these words.

_____

_____

If you need help with the spelling words,
look back at page 9.

CHAPTER
TWO

Friends

Words to Learn

Write each word in the blank.

1. pal _____

2. buddy _____

3. grin _____

4. funny _____

5. group _____

6. team _____

7. games _____

8. toys _____

9. inside _____

10. outside _____

Write your hardest words again here:

_____

_____

_____

Merry-Go-Round

Start at any letter and move around the circle, either forward or backward, to find one of your spelling words. Circle the first letter. Write the word under each circle.

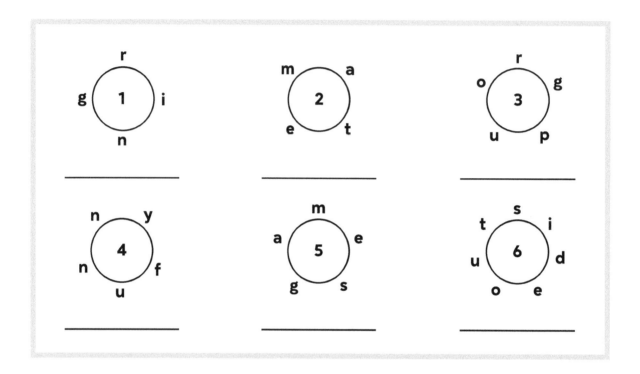

Scrambles

Write the correct spelling word for each set of scrambled letters.

1. n r i g   __ __ __ __

2. u p o r g   __ __ __ __ __

3. s y o t   __ __ __ __

4. n u n y f   __ __ __ __ __

5. s m e a g   __ __ __ __ __

6. s t i o d u e   __ __ __ __ __ __ __

7. d u b y d   __ __ __ __ __
₃

8. d i s e n i   __ __ __ __ __ __

Write a sentence using one of these words.

_____

_____

If you need help with the spelling words,
look back at page 17.

Box Stop

Write your words from the box in each blank. You will not use all the words.

group	inside	grin	outside	pal
games	buddy	funny	toys	team

1. What two words have almost the same meaning as "friend"?

    _____   _____

2. What two words can mean "more than one person"?

    _____   _____

3. What two words are opposites?

    _____   _____

4. What two things can you use when you play?

    _____   _____

Word Search

Circle each word you find in the word search. Words may go up, down, or across, both backward and forward. Write each word as you find it.

t	f	e	d	i	s	t	u	o
h	s	z	f	s	y	o	t	a
l	g	i	i	n	s	i	d	e
e	r	g	u	y	n	n	u	f
s	o	r	e	q	l	m	v	t
p	u	i	a	j	k	n	r	e
a	p	n	w	y	v	r	l	a
l	w	g	a	m	e	s	n	m
x	y	y	d	d	u	b	m	i

inside _____

outside _____

team _____

games _____

funny _____

grin _____

group _____

buddy _____

pal _____

toys _____

Tic-Tac-Toe

Circle every word spelled correctly. Draw a line across three of them to score a tic-tac-toe. Write the misspelled words correctly in the blanks.

buddie	gruop	games
team	grin	inside
toyes	funy	otside

_____

_____

_____

Places, Please

Add each of your spelling words to this puzzle. Use the letters shown to help you.
Cross off each word after you put it in the puzzle. Write your word again in the blank.

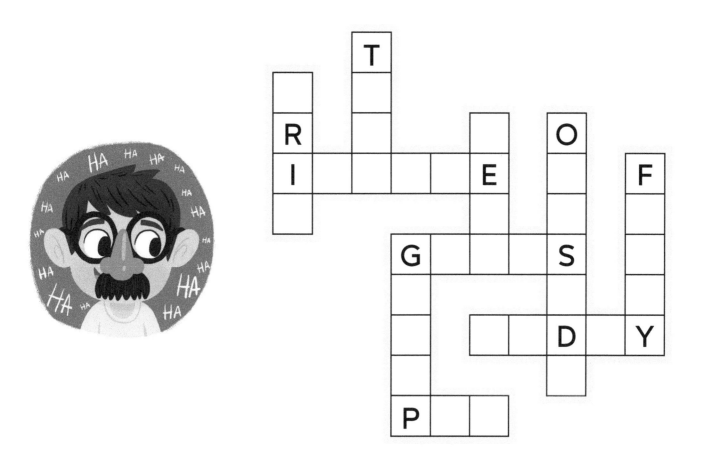

funny _____

grin _____

group _____

team _____

toys _____

games _____

inside _____

outside _____

pal _____

buddy _____

Words to Learn

Write each word in the blank.

1. children _____

2. birthday _____

3. party _____

4. balloon _____

5. talk _____

6. laugh _____

7. listen _____

8. joke _____

9. give _____

10. friend _____

Write your hardest words again here:

_____

_____

_____

Match Up

When writing, some letters reach above the line and some go below it. Look at the shapes to help you find the right spelling word and write it in the matching shape.

| joke | give | talk | laugh | listen | party |

1.

2.

3.

4.

5.
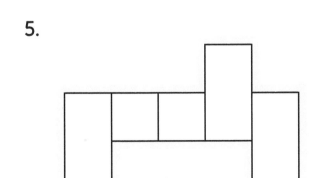

6.
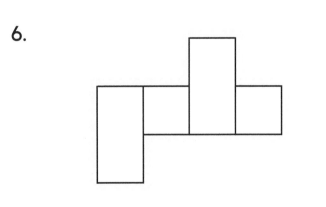

Scrambles

Write the correct spelling word for each set of scrambled letters.

1. k a t l   __ __ __ __

2. o k j e   __ __ __ __

3. e d i f r n   __ __ __ __ __ __

4. t a y r p   __ __ __ __ __

5. h u g a l   __ __ __ __ __

6. s i l n e t   __ __ __ __ __ __

7. l d e h i n c r   __ __ __ __ __ __ __ __

8. o n l a o b l   __ __ __ __ __ __ __

Write a sentence using one of these words.

_____

_____

If you need help with the spelling words, look back at page 24.

Be Choosy!

Choose the best answer and circle it. Write the word in the blank.

1. On my next _____, I will be seven years old.

   joke   friend   birthday

2. I can hear lots of _____ playing in the park.

   listen   children   friend

3. It's fun to tell a good _____.

   joke   laugh   party

4. I will _____ my friend a gift at his party.

   laugh   give   joke

5. When I let go of the _____, it floated in the air.

   friend   balloon   party

Merry-Go-Round

Start at any letter and move around the circle, either forward or backward, to find one of your spelling words. Circle the first letter. Write the word under each circle.

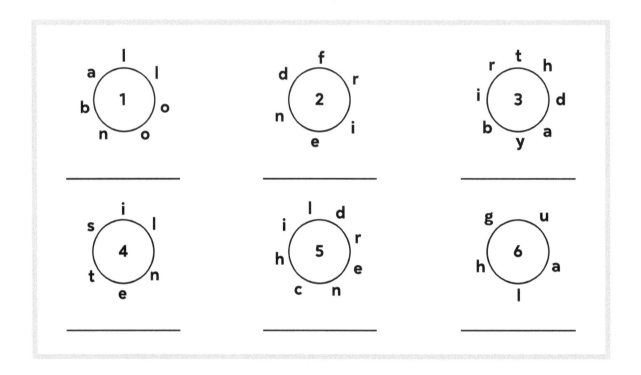

Box Stop

Write your words from the box in each blank. You will not use all the words.

party	listen	give	birthday	balloon
laugh	children	friend	talk	joke

1. I like to play with my best _____.

2. I always _____ when I hear a funny _____.

3. Can you please _____ to what I am saying?

4. I will plan a _____ for my pal's _____.

5. I will _____ to you on the phone soon.

Missing Letters

Add the missing letters to finish the spelling words.

1. ___ a ___ ___ y

2. l ___ ___ ___ h

3. g ___ ___ e

4. b ___ ___ t ___ d ___ ___

5. f r ___ 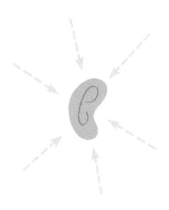 ___ d

6. l i ___ ___ ___ n

7. t ___ ___ k

8. c h ___ ___ ___ ___ e ___

Write a sentence using one of these words.

_____

_____

If you need help with the spelling words,
look back at page 24.

30

CHAPTER

THREE

- - - - -

At School

Words to Learn

Write each word in the blank.

1. add _____

2. count _____

3. write _____

4. spell _____

5. read _____

6. draw _____

7. paint _____

8. think _____

9. work _____

10. learn _____

Write your hardest words again here:

_____

_____

_____

Match Up

When writing, some letters reach above the line and some go below it. Look at the shapes to help you find the right spelling word and write it in the matching shape.

count	paint	think	learn	write	spell

1.

2.

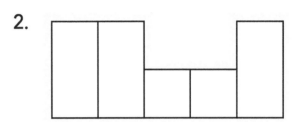

3.

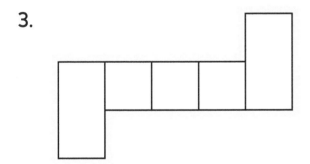

4.

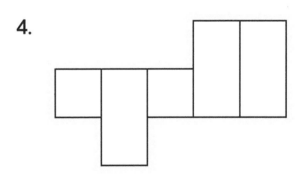

5.

6.

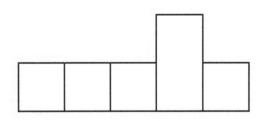

Letter Slides

Slide letters from the first word down to the second using the arrow. Keep going, sliding letters from each word down to the word below it, until you have reached the end of each slide.

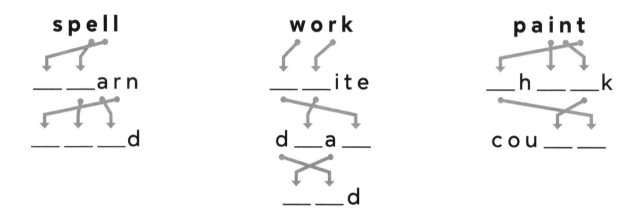

s p e l l

_ _ a r n

_ _ _ _ d

w o r k

_ _ _ i t e

d _ _ a _

_ _ _ d

p a i n t

_ h _ _ _ k

c o u _ _ _

Write a sentence using one of these words.

_____

_____

Tic-Tac-Toe

Circle every word spelled correctly. Draw a line across three of them to score a tic-tac-toe. Write the misspelled words correctly on the lines below.

read	cont	drau
spel	add	werk
lern	write	paint

_____

_____

_____

123

Be Choosy!

Choose the best answer and circle it. Write the word in the blank.

1. My sister and I like to _____ books together.

    add   think   read

2. I want to _____ new spelling words.

    count   learn   work

3. My little brother can _____ to 10.

    paint   write   count

4. I can _____ 10 plus 20.

    add   think   spell

5. If we _____ hard now, we can play games later.

    paint   work   draw

Crack the Code

Use the code provided to find your spelling words. Write each letter as you solve it.

1. $+$ ♦ 7 2 ▲

    —— —— —— —— ——

2. 3 6 Ý ★

    —— —— —— ——
    5

3. { 1 □ 2 $+$

    —— —— —— —— ——

4. ★ 1 6 ▲

    —— —— —— ——

5. 4 5 Ý 6 2

    —— —— —— —— ——

6. ★ 6 7 $+$ 5

    —— —— —— —— ——

1 = o	♦ = h
2 = n	★ = w
3 = d	Ý = a
4 = l	$+$ = t
5 = e	□ = u
6 = r	{ = c
7 = i	▲ = k

Places, Please

Add each of your spelling words to this puzzle. Use the letters shown to help you.
Cross off each word after you put it in the puzzle. Write your word again in the blank.

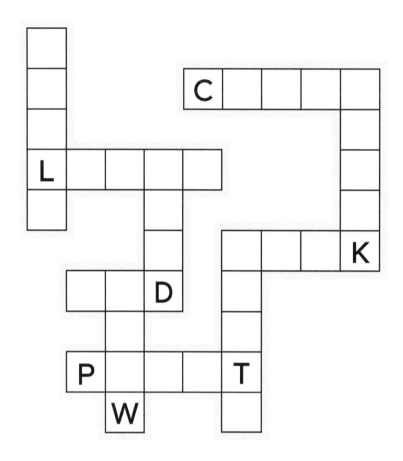

learn _____

work _____

paint _____

draw _____

read _____

spell _____

write _____

count _____

add _____

think _____

Words to Learn

Write each word in the blank.

1. paper _____

2. pencil _____

3. desk _____

4. shelf _____

5. class _____

6. teacher _____

7. grade _____

8. study _____

9. backpack _____

10. lunchroom _____

Write your hardest words again here:

_____

_____

_____

Missing Letters

Add the missing letters to finish the spelling words.

1. p __ n __ __ l

2. t __ __ __ __ e r

3. s __ __ __ f

4. s __ __ d __

5. __ a __ e __

6. __ e __ __

7. b __ __ __ p __ __ __

8. l __ n __ __ r __ __ m

Write a sentence using one of these words.

_____

_____

If you need help with the spelling words,
look back at page 39.

Merry-Go-Round

Start at any letter and move around the circle, either forward or backward, to find one of your spelling words. Circle the first letter. Write the word under each circle.

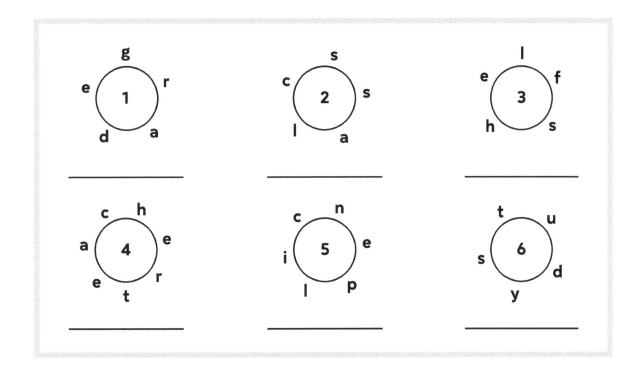

_____

_____

_____

_____

_____

_____

Box Stop

Write your words from the box in each blank. You will not use all the words.

shelf	teacher	pencil	backpack	paper
study	class	grade	desk	lunchroom

1. What word describes all the students in your room? _____

2. What three words tell where you can put your books?

   _____   _____   _____

3. Who helps you learn new things? _____

4. What word tells the place where you can eat? _____

5. What word tells what you do to learn facts? _____

6. What can you sharpen? _____

Word Search

Circle each word you find in the word search. Words may go up, down, or across, both backward and forward. Write each word as you find it.

s	q	z	l	i	c	n	e	p
h	s	s	b	k	j	v	z	j
e	t	y	a	e	d	a	r	g
l	u	n	c	h	r	o	o	m
f	d	w	k	w	v	a	l	c
n	y	d	p	g	z	a	w	l
a	i	p	a	p	e	r	j	a
r	e	h	c	a	e	t	q	s
p	y	e	k	s	e	d	g	s

lunchroom _____

backpack _____

class _____

grade _____

teacher _____

desk _____

study _____

pencil _____

paper _____

shelf _____

Scrambles

Write the correct spelling word for each set of scrambled letters.

1. c l i p n e   __ __ __ __ __ __

2. e h l f s   __ __ __ __ __

3. d a g e r   __ __ __ __ __

4. s k e d   __ __ __ __

5. c r a t e h e   __ __ __ __ __ __ __

6. a p p r e   __ __ __ __ __

7. a a b c c k k p   __ __ __ __ __ __ __ __

8. s c l a s   __ __ __ __ __

Write a sentence using one of these words.

_____

_____

If you need help with the spelling words,
look back at page 39.

Follow the Clues

Write the spelling words that fit each clue. There will be several answers at first. You will write some spelling words more than once. For the last clue, there will be just one word. Which word will it be?

lunchroom	backpack	study	paper	grade
pencil	teacher	shelf	class	study

1. Six things inside a classroom

   _____   _____   _____

   _____   _____   _____

2. Three things inside a classroom that are easy to carry

   _____   _____   _____

3. Two things inside a classroom that are easy to carry and used when writing   _____   _____

4. One thing inside a classroom that is easy to carry, used for writing, and can be folded _____

CHAPTER

FOUR

Animals

Words to Learn

Write each word in the blank.

1. dog   _____
2. fish   _____
3. frog   _____
4. duck   _____
5. chicken _____
6. kitten _____
7. rabbit _____
8. sheep   _____
9. goat   _____
10. horse _____

Write your hardest words again here:

_____

_____

_____

Letter Slides

Slide letters from the first word down to the second using the arrow. Keep going, sliding letters from each word down to the word below it, until you have reached the end of each slide.

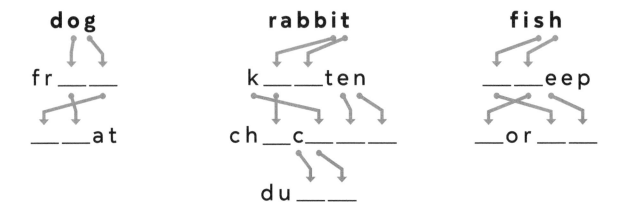

Write a sentence using one of these words.

_____

_____

Match Up

When writing, some letters reach above the line and some go below it. Look at the shapes to help you find the right spelling word and write it in the matching shape.

frog   horse   rabbit   kitten   duck   sheep

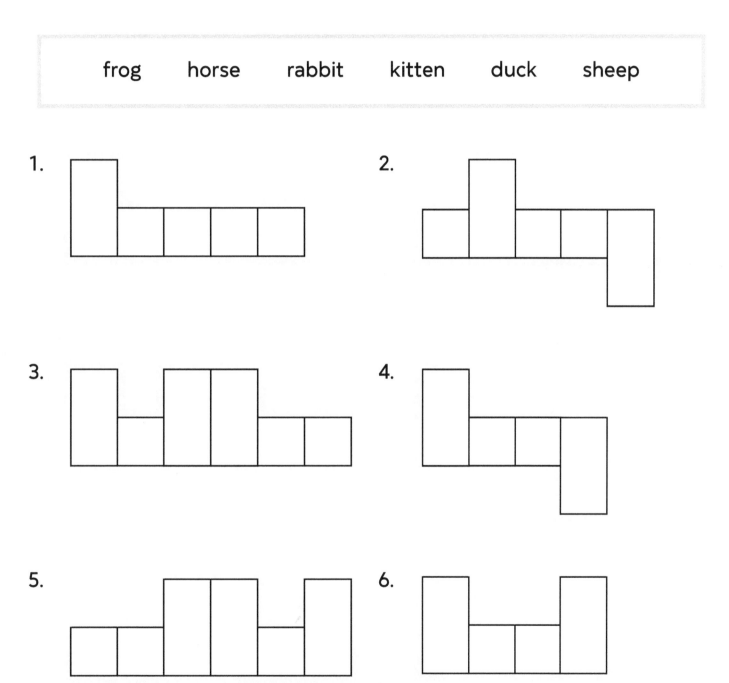

1.

2.

3.

4.

5.

6.

Be Choosy!

Choose the best answer and circle it. Write the word in the blank.

1. This _____ lays an egg every day.

   chicken   fish   kitten

2. A puppy grows up to be a _____.

   frog   rabbit   dog

3. A lamb grows up to be a _____.

   horse   sheep   duck

4. A _____ grows up to be a cat.

   dog   kitten   goat

5. A _____ says, "Quack!"

   goat   duck   rabbit

Tic-Tac-Toe

Circle every word spelled correctly. Draw a line across three of them to score a tic-tac-toe. Write the misspelled words correctly on the lines below.

kiten	chiken	sheep
rabit	frog	gote
duck	fish	shepe

_____

_____

_____

Follow the Clues

Write the spelling words that fit each clue. There will be several answers at first. You will write some spelling words more than once. For the last clue, there will be just one word. Which word will it be?

dog	fish	frog	duck	chicken
kitten	rabbit	sheep	goat	horse

1. Six animals with four legs

    _____   _____   _____

    _____   _____   _____

2. Two animals with four legs that are spelled with six letters

    _____   _____

3. One animal with four legs, spelled with six letters, and that has a

    short, furry tail   _____

Missing Letters

Add the missing letters to finish the spelling words.

1. h __ O s e
   7

2. __ __ i c __ __ n

3. d __ __ __

4. __ i __ __

5. __ __ __ g

6. __ o __

7. k __ __ __ e __

8. __ h __ __ __

Write a sentence using one of these words.

_____

_____

If you need help with the spelling words,
look back at page 47.

Words to Learn

Write each word in the blank.

1. whale   _____

2. snail   _____

3. shark   _____

4. lion   _____

5. tiger   _____

6. camel   _____

7. snake   _____

8. goose   _____

9. ladybug   _____

10. butterfly   _____

Write your hardest words again here:

_____

_____

Merry-Go-Round

Start at any letter and move around the circle, either forward or backward, to find one of your spelling words. Circle the first letter. Write the word under each circle.

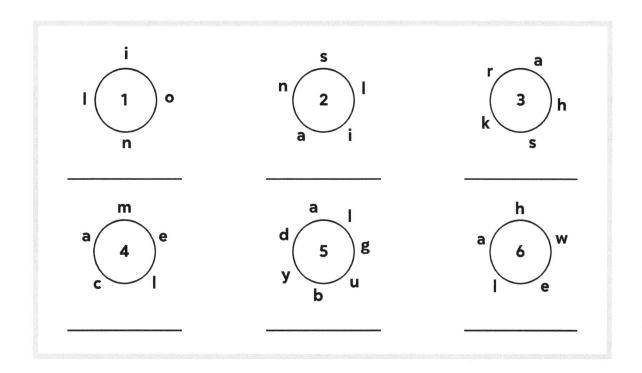

Scrambles

Write the correct spelling word for each set of scrambled letters.

1. m e c a l   __ __ __ __ __

2. g r i t e   __ __ __ __ __

3. o s e o g   __ __ __ __ __

4. k e n a s   __ __ __ __ __

5. g l y a b u d   __ __ __ __ __ __ __

6. l a w e h   __ __ __ __ __

7. r h a s k   __ __ __ __ __

8. t r u f b y e l t   __ __ __ __ __ __ __ __ __

Write a sentence using one of these words.

_____

_____

If you need help with the spelling words, look back at page 54.

Box Stop

Write your words from the box in each blank. You will not use all the words.

whale	shark	snail	tiger	lion
camel	snake	goose	ladybug	butterfly

1. What two words rhyme?

    _____   _____

2. What two words share three of the same letters in the same order?

    _____   _____

3. What three animals can fly?

    _____   _____   _____

4. Which two animals always live in the water?

    _____   _____

5. Which animal would you most like to ride?

    _____

Match Up

When writing, some letters reach above the line and some go below it. Look at the shapes to help you find the right spelling word and write it in the matching shape.

camel   tiger   lion   goose   snake   whale

1.

2.

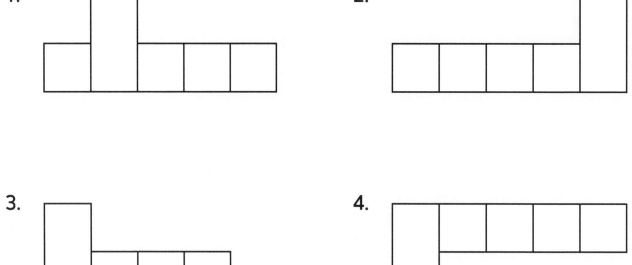

3.

4.

5.

6.

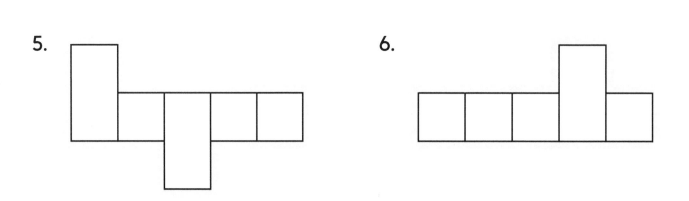

Word Search

Circle each word you find in the word search. Words may go up, down, or across, both backward and forward. Write each word as you find it.

l	c	e	l	e	n	o	i	l
i	g	l	e	s	h	a	r	k
a	e	a	m	o	v	k	y	d
n	e	h	a	o	e	v	g	b
s	l	w	c	g	t	h	p	v
y	l	f	r	e	t	t	u	b
t	i	g	e	r	h	u	t	r
u	c	l	a	d	y	b	u	g
j	p	q	g	e	k	a	n	s

lion _____

tiger _____

camel _____

goose _____

snake _____

snail _____

shark _____

whale _____

ladybug _____

butterfly _____

Crack the Code

Use the code to find your spelling words. Write each letter as you solve it.

1. Ω 6 ¶ 5 7

   __ __ __ __ __

2. → ¥ ¥ Ω 3

   __ __ __ __ __

3. 1 ✳ ¶ 7 3

   __ __ __ __ __

4. Ω 6 ¶ 4 3

   __ __ __ __ __

   8

5. 2 5 → 3 @

   __ __ __ __ __

6. Ω ✳ ¶ @ 4

   __ __ __ __ __

1 = w	@ = r
2 = t	¶ = a
3 = e	→ = g
4 = k	¥ = o
5 = i	Ω = s
6 = n	✳ = h
7 = l	

CHAPTER

FIVE

In the Park

Words to Learn

Write each word in the blank.

1. grass   _____

2. trees   _____

3. water   _____

4. pond   _____

5. pool   _____

6. air   _____

7. walk   _____

8. skip   _____

9. jump   _____

10. climb   _____

Write your hardest words again here:

_____

_____

_____

Letter Slides

Slide letters from the first word down to the second using the arrow. Keep going, sliding letters from each word down to the word below it, until you have reached the end of each slide.

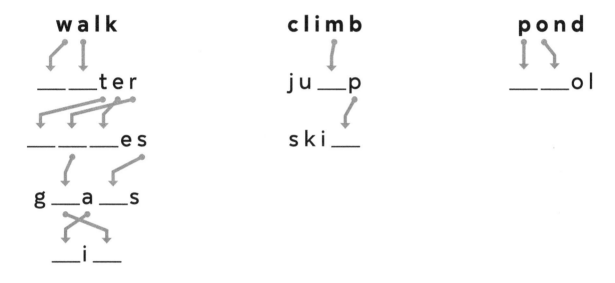

Write a sentence using one of these words.

_____

_____

Be Choosy!

Choose the best answer and circle it. Write the word in the blank.

1. We need to drink _____ every day.

   water   grass   air

2. How high can you _____ in a tree?

   walk   path   climb

3. I like to swim in the indoor _____.

   pond   pool   grass

4. It's fun to go on a _____ with a friend.

   walk   jump   air

5. It was hard for me to learn to _____.

   trees   skip   pool

Box Stop

Write your words from the box in each blank. You will not use all the words.

walk	trees	water	pond	jump
air	grass	skip	pool	climb

1. What four words tell what you can do at the park?

   _____   _____

   _____   _____

2. Which word describes the thing you most like to do?

   _____

3. What two words name things that hold water?

   _____   _____

4. What two things grow?

   _____   _____

5. Write a sentence that uses two words from the box.

   _____

   _____

Tic-Tac-Toe

Circle every word spelled correctly. Draw a line across three of them to score a tic-tac-toe. Write the misspelled words correctly in the blanks.

clim	scip	water
trees	air	jump
wak	pol	gras

_____

_____

_____

Scrambles

Write the correct spelling word for each set of scrambled letters.

1. k a l w   ___ ___ ___ ___

2. s a g s r   ___ ___ ___ ___ ___

3. m u p j   ___ ___ ___ ___

4. t r a w e   ___ ___ ___ ___ ___

5. l o p o   ___ ___ ___ ___

6. n o d p   ___ ___  ___ ___

7. b l i m c   ___ ___ ___ ___ ___

8. k s p i   ___ ___ ___ ___

Write a sentence using one of these words.

_____

_____

If you need help with the spelling words,
look back at page 62.

Letter Sense

Add the missing letters to your spelling words so each sentence makes sense.

1. The warm summer ___ ___ r feels nice.

2. We have shade from the tall t ___ ___ ___ s.

3. Do you like to play ___ ___ ___ p rope?

4. Dad can catch fish in our ___ ___ n ___.

5. It is time to mow our g ___ ___ ___ ___ again.

6. W ___ ___ ___ ___ is good for many things.

If you need help with the spelling words,
look back at page 62.

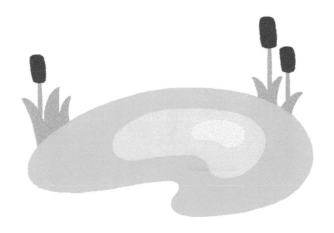

Write each word in the blank.

1. birds   _____

2. flowers   _____

3. path   _____

4. slide   _____

5. sandbox   _____

6. playground   _____

7. kites   _____

8. wind   _____

9. camping   _____

10. sunshine   _____

Write your hardest words again here:

_____

_____

_____

Merry-Go-Round

Start at any letter and move around the circle, either forward or backward, to find one of your spelling words. Circle the first letter. Write the word under each circle.

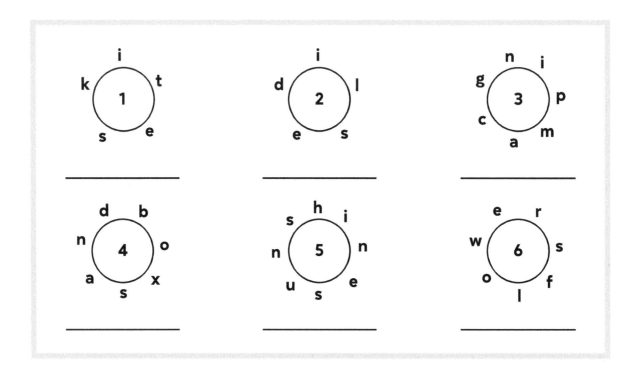

1. i k t s e (circle 1)

2. i d l e s (circle 2)

3. n i g p c m a (circle 3)

4. d b n o a x s (circle 4)

5. h i s n n u s e (circle 5)

6. e r w s o f l (circle 6)

_____

_____

_____

_____

_____

_____

Word Search

Circle each word you find in the word search. Words may go up, down, across, or diagonally, both backward and forward. Write each word as you find it.

p	c	g	r	k	i	t	e	s	c	d
u	l	g	n	i	p	m	a	c	k	x
b	d	a	x	r	j	f	l	z	o	x
b	i	m	y	i	q	i	b	b	g	f
f	x	r	s	g	o	b	d	y	h	l
u	m	r	d	b	r	n	t	s	t	o
d	n	i	w	s	a	o	e	q	a	w
z	h	l	k	s	w	d	u	q	p	e
s	u	n	s	h	i	n	e	n	r	r
l	r	l	y	l	v	w	b	t	d	s
a	n	g	s	w	e	g	a	i	h	o

birds _____

flowers _____

path _____

slide _____

sandbox _____

playground _____

kites _____

wind _____

camping _____

sunshine _____

Be Choosy!

Choose the best answer and circle it. Write the word in the blank.

1. There are many things to play on at the _____.

   slide   sandbox   playground

2. My kite will fly well if there is some _____.

   sunshine   birds   wind

3. Let's walk along this _____.

   camping   path   sandbox

4. My little sister likes to play with toys and trucks in the _____.

   kites   sandbox   path

5. I enjoy smelling the lovely _____ at the park.

   flowers   wind   birds

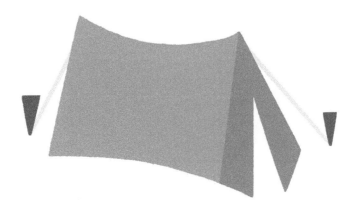

Crack the Code

Use the code to find your spelling words. Write each letter as you solve it.

1. _ € 2 § ♥

   ___ ___ ___ ___ ___

2. 3 € 1 §

   ___ ___ ___ ___

3. ♥ 7 € § °

   ___ ___ ___ ___ ___

4. 4 7 6 3 ° 2 ♥

   ___ ___ ___ ___ ___ ___ ___

5. 5 € ? ° ♥

   ___ ___ ___ ___ ___
   10

6. ♥ 8 1 § _ 6 ✳

   ___ ___ ___ ___ ___ ___ ___

1 = n	♥ = s
2 = r	? = t
3 = w	_ = b
4 = f	€ = i
5 = k	° = e
6 = o	✳ = x
7 = l	§ = d
8 = a	

Follow the Clues

Write the spelling words that fit each clue. There will be several answers at first. You will write some spelling words more than once. For the last clue, there will be just one word. Which word will it be?

sunshine	wind	sandbox	playground	camping
kites	flowers	birds	slide	path

1. Three words that mean there is *more than one*

    _____   _____   _____

2. Two things that fly

    _____   _____

3. One thing that flies and is not made by people _____

Write a sentence that uses any word from the box.

_____

_____

Letter Sense

Add the missing letters to your spelling words so each sentence makes sense.

1. I like to go c___ ___ ___ i ___ ___ with my aunt and uncle.

2. It's nice to be out in the s ___ ___ s ___ ___ ___ e.

3. The p___ ___ ___ g ___ ___ ___ ___d by my house has lots of swings.

4. It also has one big s ___ ___ ___ e.

5. My friends and I like to play together in the ___ ___ ___ d ___ ___ x.

6. There is no ___ ___ ___ d, so we cannot fly our k ___ ___ ___ ___.

> **If you need help with the spelling words, look back at page 69.**

CHAPTER

SIX

- - - - -

Colors and Numbers

Words to Learn

Write each word in the blank.

1. red _____

2. blue _____

3. green _____

4. yellow _____

5. white _____

6. black _____

7. gold _____

8. brown _____

9. orange _____

10. purple _____

Write your hardest words again here:

_____

_____

_____

Match Up

When writing, some letters reach above the line and some go below it. Look at the shapes to help you find the right spelling word and write it in the matching shape.

green   white   black   brown   orange   purple

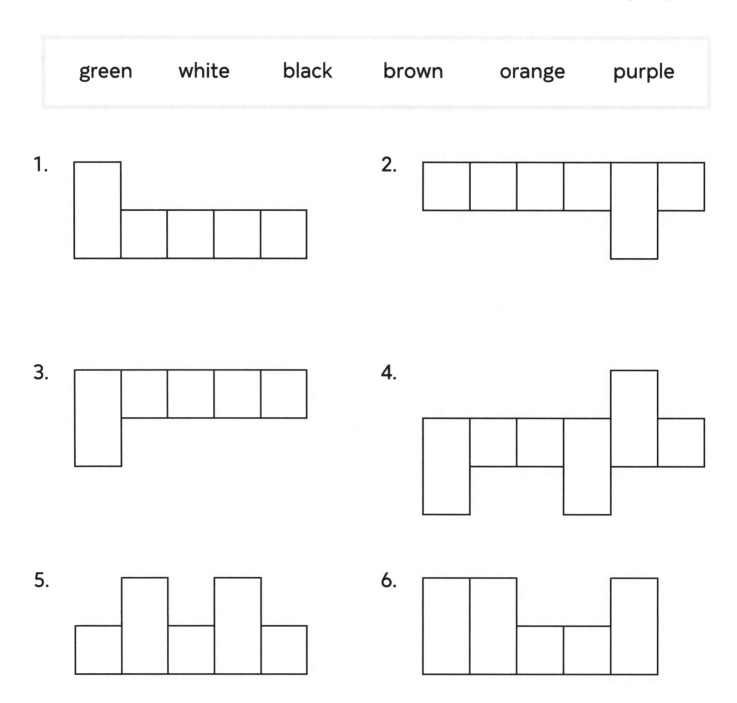

Scrambles

Write the correct spelling word for each set of scrambled letters.

1. d e r   __ __ __

2. l e w o l y   __ __ __ __ __ __

3. l o g d   __ __ __ __

4. u l e b   __ __ __ __

5. l u p p r e   __ __ __ __ __ __

6. t w e i h   __ __ __ __ __

7. g r o a n e   __ __ __ __ __ __

8. k a l c b   __ __ __ __ __

Write a sentence using one of these words.

_____

_____

If you need help with the spelling words,
look back at page 77.

Box Stop

Write your words from the box in each blank. You will not use all the words.

brown	black	white	blue	orange
red	gold	green	purple	yellow

1. The color of the hidden coins in the mystery at the beginning of this

   book _____

2. The color of the letters in this book _____

3. Two colors you might use to color the sun

   _____ _____

4. The color of snow _____

5. The color of the sky on a clear day _____

6. The color of mud _____

7. The color you get when you mix red and blue _____

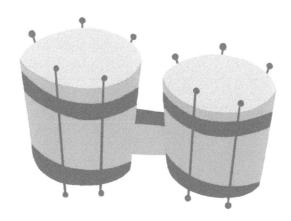

Tic-Tac-Toe

Circle every color that is spelled correctly. Draw a line across three of them to score a tic-tac-toe. Write the misspelled words correctly in the blanks.

read	yelow	black
blew	white	perple
green	broun	gold

_____

_____

_____

Missing Letters

Add the missing letters to finish the spelling words.

1. b 〇 ___ ___ e
   11

2. g ___ ___ ___ n

3. ___ ___ ___ d

4. b ___ ___ ___ n

5. ___ ___ a n ___ ___

6. p ___ ___ p ___ ___

7. ___ e ___ ___ o ___

8. ___ h ___ ___ e

Write a sentence using one of these words.

_____

_____

If you need help with the spelling words,
look back at page 77.

Places, Please

Add each of your spelling words to this puzzle. Use the letters shown to help you.
Cross off each word after you put it in the puzzle. Write your word again in the blank.

red _____

blue _____

green _____

yellow _____

white _____

black _____

gold _____

brown _____

orange _____

purple _____

Words to Learn

Write each word in the blank.

1. zero   _____

2. four   _____

3. five   _____

4. six   _____

5. seven   _____

6. eight   _____

7. nine   _____

8. ten   _____

9. eleven   _____

10. twelve   _____

Write your hardest words again here:

_____

_____

_____

Be Choosy!

Choose the best answer for each number pattern and circle it. Write the word in the blank.

1. One, two, three, . . . _____

   four   five   six

2. Ten, nine, eight, . . . _____

   nine   seven   six

3. Two, four, six, . . . _____

   eight   ten   eleven

4. Eight, nine, ten, . . . _____

   twelve   eleven   seven

5. Three, two, one, . . . _____

   four   five   zero

6. One, three, five, . . . _____

   six   seven   four

Word Search

Circle each word you find in the word search. Words may go up, down, across, or diagonally, both backward and forward. Write each word as you find it.

b	v	x	p	n	e	v	e	s
o	e	f	i	e	v	x	i	s
r	s	l	w	u	i	f	w	e
e	k	t	e	d	n	g	x	s
z	o	m	w	v	y	i	h	o
e	f	z	j	e	e	j	n	t
r	m	o	a	m	l	n	l	e
n	e	t	u	f	i	v	e	s
q	n	a	r	r	l	z	e	t

zero _____

four _____

five _____

six _____

seven _____

eight _____

nine _____

ten _____

eleven _____

twelve _____

Letter Sense

Add the missing letters to your spelling words so each sentence makes sense.

1. I started with three apples. I gave them all away. So, I had

   ___ e ___ ___ apples left.

2. Today is May 1. My birthday is May 5. I will wait f ___ ___ ___ more

   days for my birthday.

3. Our chickens laid five eggs yesterday and four more today. In all,

   they laid ___ ___ ___ e eggs in two days.

4. There are ___ ___ ___ ___ n days in one week.

5. Ten plus two equals t ___ ___ ___ ___ ___.

6. I have ten spelling words. Only two of them are tricky, so

   ___ ___ ___ ___ t of them are easy!

   12

10   12

Letter Slides

Slide letters from the first word down to the second using the arrow. Keep going, sliding letters from each word down to the word below it, until you have reached the end of each slide.

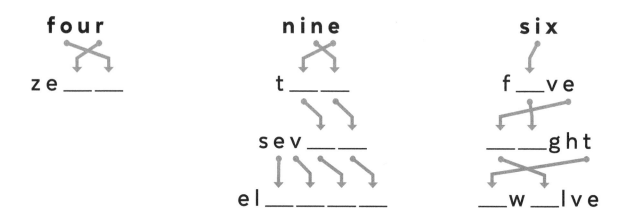

Write a sentence using one of these words.

_____

_____

Follow the Clues

Write the spelling number words that fit each clue. There will be several answers at first. You will write some spelling words more than once. For the last clue, there will be just one word. Which word will it be?

zero	four	five	six	seven
eight	nine	ten	eleven	twelve

1. Four odd numbers greater than four

   _____ _____ _____ _____

2. Two odd numbers greater than four, spelled with five or more letters

   _____ _____

3. One odd number greater than four, spelled with five or more letters, and written with two digits _____

Number Chart

Write the missing number words in this number chart.

0	
1	one
2	two
3	three
4	
5	
6	
7	
8	
9	
10	
11	
12	
13	thirteen
14	fourteen

CHAPTER
SEVEN

Feelings

Words to Learn

Write each word in the blank.

1. glad _____

2. sad _____

3. happy _____

4. scared _____

5. silly _____

6. safe _____

7. mean _____

8. lost _____

9. angry _____

10. strong _____

Write your hardest words again here:

_____

_____

_____

Merry-Go-Round

Start at any letter and move around the circle, either forward or backward, to find one of your spelling words. Circle the first letter. Write the word under each circle.

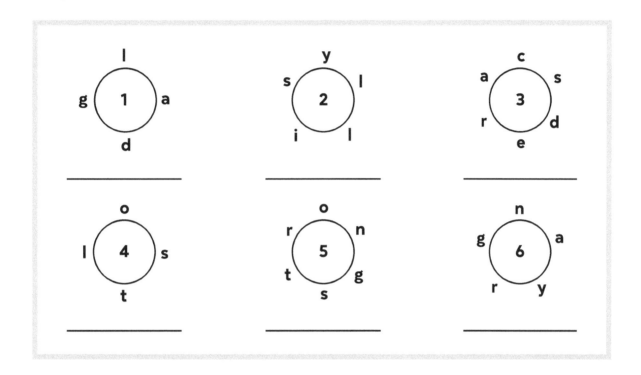

1. l g (1) a d

2. y s (2) l i l

3. c a (3) s r e d

4. o l (4) s t

5. o r (5) n t ( ) g s

6. n g (6) a r y

Box Stop

Write your words from the box in each blank. You will not use all the words.

glad	angry	happy	scared	silly
safe	lost	mean	sad	strong

1. What two words rhyme? _____ _____

2. What word has almost the same meaning as "happy"? _____

3. What word has the same meaning as "mad"? _____

4. What word has the same meaning as "funny"? _____

5. What word tells how you might feel if you were alone during a storm?

   _____

6. Write a sentence about a time when you felt strong.

   _____

   _____

Match Up

When writing, some letters reach above the line and some go below it. Look at the shapes to help you find the right spelling word and write it in the matching shape.

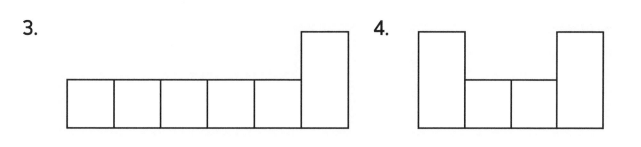

lost   strong   angry   safe   scared   silly

1.

2.

3.

4.

5.

6.

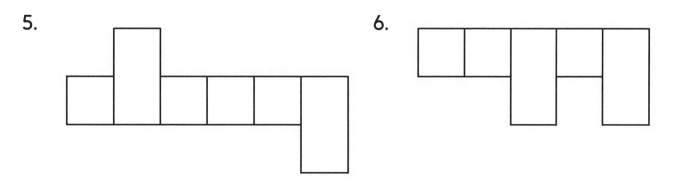

Scrambles

Write the correct spelling word for each set of scrambled letters.

1. p a p h y   _ _ _ _ _

2. s o l t   _ _ _ _

3. l a g d   _ _ _ _

4. n y a g r   _ _ _ _ _

5. i s l y l   _ _ _ _ _

6. a s d   _ _ _

7. c e r d a s   _ _ _ _ _ _

8. g r o s n t   _ _ _ _ _ _

Write a sentence using one of these words.

_____

_____

If you need help with the spelling words,
look back at page 92.

Letter Sense

Add the missing letters to your spelling words so each sentence makes sense.

1. I was g ___ ___ ___ when my grandpa came to my house.

2. We were all ___ ___ d when he left.

3. My mother makes sure we stay ___ ___ ___ e when we go to the mall.

4. She does not want us to get l ___ ___ ___ .

5. My friend's dog is m ___ ___ .
   13

6. When the dog barks, I feel s ___ ___ ___ ___ ___.

> If you need help with the spelling words,
> look back at page 92.

Places, Please

Add each of your spelling words to this puzzle. Use the letters shown to help you. Cross off each word after you put it in the puzzle. Write your word again in the blank.

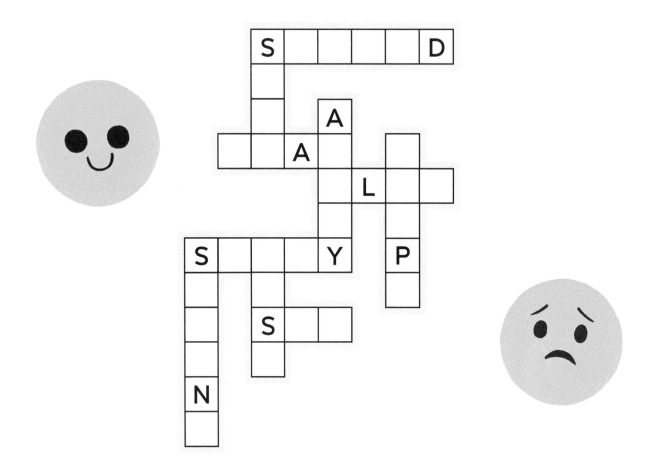

glad _____

sad _____

happy _____

scared _____

safe _____

strong _____

lost _____

mean _____

angry _____

silly _____

Words to Learn

Write each word in the blank.

1. sorry _____

2. cross _____

3. joyful _____

4. thankful _____

5. hurt _____

6. proud _____

7. bored _____

8. gloomy _____

9. afraid _____

10. hopeful _____

Write your hardest words again here:

_____

_____

_____

Letter Slides

Slide letters from the first word down to the second using the arrow. Keep going, sliding letters from each word down to the word below it, until you have reached the end of each slide.

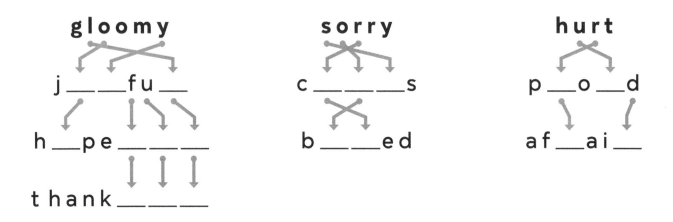

gloomy

j _____ fu __

h __ pe _____

t h a n k _____

sorry

c _____ s

b _____ e d

hurt

p __ o __ d

a f __ a i __

Write a sentence using one of these words.

_____

_____

Be Choosy!

Choose the best answer and circle it. Write the word in the blank.

1. You did your best work and I am very _____ of you!

   proud   cross   afraid

2. I cannot find anything to do, so I am very _____.

   hurt   bored   sorry

3. We are _____ that the day will be sunny tomorrow.

   gloomy   cross   hopeful

4. My dog feels _____ when there are storms.

   joyful   afraid   thankful

5. Sometimes I get _____ when I don't feel well.

   cross   proud   joyful

6. I am very _____ for your help!

   thankful   sorry   afraid

Tic-Tac-Toe

Circle every word spelled correctly. Draw a line across three of them to score a tic-tac-toe. Write the misspelled words correctly on the lines below.

bord	afriad	thankful
glomy	hert	proud
sorry	hopful	joyful

_____

_____

_____

Word Search

Circle each word you find in the word search. Words may go up, down, across, or diagonally, both backward and forward. Write each word as you find it.

y	t	i	o	g	r	t	r	u	h
u	c	h	s	o	r	r	y	c	s
w	e	r	a	v	m	z	r	d	g
d	d	q	o	n	d	i	a	e	w
d	u	t-	o	s	k	h	z	r	l
h	o	m	z	i	s	f	y	o	u
h	r	h	u	p	v	y	u	b	f
l	p	h	o	p	e	f	u	l	y
d	i	a	r	f	a	f	k	b	o
g	l	o	o	m	y	s	p	s	j

joyful _____

thankful _____

hopeful _____

gloomy _____

afraid _____

cross _____

bored _____

proud _____

sorry _____

hurt _____

Letter Sense

Add the missing letters to your spelling words so each sentence makes sense.

1. When you are full of joy, you are ___ ___ ___ ___ ___ l.

2. I am so ___ ___ ___ ___ y that I ___ ___ r ___ your feelings!

3. It has been cloudy all week and I feel g ___ ___ ___ ___ ___.

4. What shall we do so we won't be b ___ ___ ___ ___?

5. We are ___ o ___ ___ ___ u ___ that we will go on a trip soon.

6. I am ___ ___ o ___ ___ of my little sister for learning to ride a scooter!

If you need help with the spelling words, look back at page 99.

Crack the Code

Use the code to find your spelling words. Write each letter as you solve it.

1. + 4 ◆ 1 2

__ __ __ __ __

2. 8 ◆ 4 ✳ 2

__ __ __ __ __

3. 3 ⇒ 4 3 □ 2

__ __ __ __ __ __

4. ♥ 6 3 4 ✳ 2

__ __ __ __ __ __

5. 7 ◆ @ ⇒ 1 5

__ __ __ __ __ __

6. ♥ ◆ 4 4 @

14 __ __ __ __ __

1 = u	+ = p
2 = d	@ = y
3 = a	□ = i
4 = r	♥ = s
5 = l	◆ = o
6 = c	⇒ = f
7 = j	✳ = e
8 = b	

CHAPTER
EIGHT

- - - - -

At Home

Words to Learn

Write each word in the blank.

1. house   _____

2. roof   _____

3. floor   _____

4. door   _____

5. stove   _____

6. sink   _____

7. room   _____

8. table   _____

9. chairs   _____

10. broom   _____

Write your hardest words again here:

_____

_____

_____

Match Up

When writing, some letters reach above the line and some go below it. Look at the shapes to help you find the right spelling word and write it in the matching shape.

| house | floor | door | table | stove | roof |

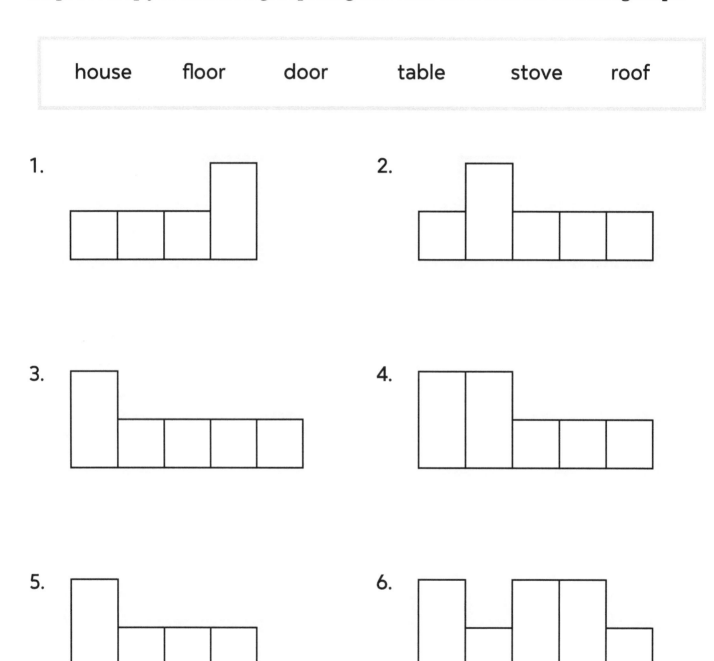

1.

2.

3.

4.

5.

6.

Box Stop

Write your words from the box in each blank. You will not use all the words.

house	roof	floor	broom	door
room	chairs	table	sink	stove

1. What two words rhyme with *zoom*?

   _____   _____

2. What word has the same meaning as *home*? _____

3. What two words rhyme with *or*?

   _____   _____

4. What word names a place where you could wash? _____

5. What word names the top of a house? _____

6. Choose one word to use in a sentence.

   _____

   _____

Merry-Go-Round

Start at any letter and move around the circle, either forward or backward, to find one of your spelling words. Circle the first letter. Write the word under each circle.

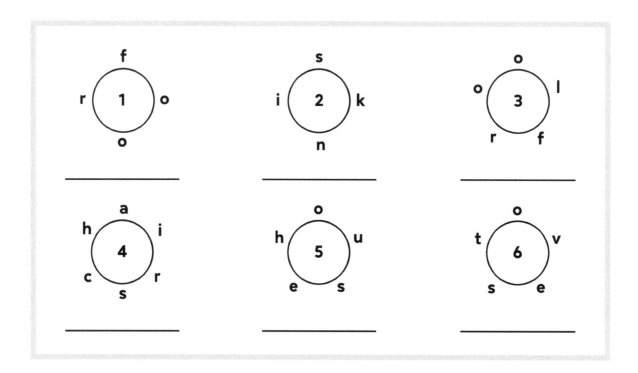

f
r (1) o
o

_____

s
i (2) k
n

_____

o
o (3) l
r   f

_____

a
h (4) i
c   r
s

_____

o
h (5) u
e   s

_____

o
t (6) v
s   e

_____

Scrambles

Write the correct spelling word for each set of scrambled letters.

1. f o r o l   __ __ __ __ __

2. o r o m b   __ __ __ __ __

3. k n i s   __ __ __ __

4. t e s v o   __ __ __ __ __

5. o o r d   __ __ __ __

6. s e u h o   __ __ __ __ __

7. s i c a h r   __ __ __ __ __ __

8. b l e a t   __ __ __ __ __

Write a sentence using one of these words.

_____

_____

If you need help with the spelling words,
look back at page 107.

Places, Please

Add each of your spelling words to this puzzle. Use the letters shown to help you. Cross off each word after you put it in the puzzle. Write your word again in the blank.

roof _____

room _____

house _____

door _____

floor _____

table _____

chairs _____

sink _____

stove _____

broom _____

Finish the Poem

Finish this rhyming poem. Use one of the spelling words from the box in each blank. If time allows, draw a picture to go with your poem on another piece of paper.

room	door	house	table	broom	floor

I know a little mouse

Who has a little ___ ___ ___ ___ ___.

He opens a little  ___ ___ ___

And walks onto the ___ ___ ___ ___ ___.

He has a little ___ ___ ___ ___ ___

To sweep each little ___ ___ ___ ___.

And now if you are able,

Please help him set his ___ ___ ___ ___ ___!

Words to Learn

Write each word in the blank.

1. carpet _____

2. lamp _____

3. sofa _____

4. couch _____

5. dishes _____

6. clock _____

7. window _____

8. bathtub _____

9. bedroom _____

10. mailbox _____

Write your hardest words again here:

_____

_____

_____

Word Search

Circle each word you find in the word search. Words may go up, down, across, or diagonally, both backward and forward. Write each word as you find it.

s	w	c	x	c	l	o	c	k	c
q	r	i	v	o	h	i	v	a	a
p	i	y	n	o	c	y	m	c	v
b	d	w	m	d	u	t	o	a	v
m	a	i	l	b	o	x	o	r	a
w	p	t	s	u	c	w	r	p	f
u	m	u	h	h	b	b	d	e	o
b	a	o	r	t	e	b	e	t	s
s	l	u	l	t	u	s	b	d	n
i	l	b	n	u	a	b	n	u	m

window _____

clock _____

sofa _____

couch _____

carpet _____

lamp _____

dishes _____

bathtub _____

bedroom _____

mailbox _____

Be Choosy!

Choose the best answer and circle it. Write the word in the blank.

1. When I'm tired I like to soak in the _____.

   carpet   bathtub   mailbox

2. My sister and I often help Dad do the _____.

   dishes   lamp   couch

3. We are going to be late. Look at the _____!

   clock   window   bedroom

4. Every day I look in the _____, hoping to find something for me.

   lamp   mailbox   sofa

5. It is cold outside, so the _____ is foggy.

   couch   carpet   window

Tic-Tac-Toe

Circle every word spelled correctly. Draw a line across three of them to score a tic-tac-toe. Write the misspelled words correctly on the lines below.

soffa	lamp	bedroom
dishs	carpet	mialbox
clock	bathub	cowch

_____

_____

_____

Letter Sense

Add the missing letters to your spelling words so each sentence makes sense.

1. Three of us can sit on the s ___ ___ ___ at one time.

2. At my house, we call this a c ___ ___ ___ ___.

3. Our floor looked old, but this new ___ ___ ___ p ___ t looks

   very nice!

4. I like to read in my b ___ ___ ___ ___ ___ m before I go to sleep.

5. Mom likes to read in the ___ ___ ___ h ___ ___ ___ !

6. Our ___ l ___ ___ ___ makes a loud ticking sound.

> If you need help with the spelling words,
> look back at page 114.

Crack the Code

Use the code to find your spelling words. Write each letter as you solve it.

1. ‡ 8 4 5 » 4

   — — — — — —

2. X £ 2 5 2 6 X

   — — — — — — —

3. 3 1 6 3 5

   — —○— — — —
   16

4. ? 8 ✳ ‡ 1 ?

   — — — — — —

5. 3 £ 7 … » 2

   — — — — — —

6. X » ‡ 7 1 1 ©

   — — — — — — —

1 = o	» = e
2 = t	✳ = n
3 = c	… = p
4 = s	‡ = d
5 = h	X = b
6 = u	£ = a
7 = r	© = m
8 = i	? = w

Finish the Poem

Finish this rhyming poem. Use one of the spelling words from the box in each blank. If time allows, draw a picture to go with your poem on another piece of paper.

| dishes | bedroom | bathtub | clock | mailbox |

All around the house there is work to do.

I will name some jobs. Here are just a few:

Ticktock, ticktock.

Don't forget to dust the ___ ___ ___ ___ ___ .

Scrub-a-dub, scrub-a-dub,

Next, let's clean the ___ ___ ___ ___ ___ ___ ___.

Use the duster and the broom

To clean up your ___ ___ ___ ___ ___ ___ ___.

Be sure there are no shoes or socks

Sitting in our ___ ___ ___ ___ ___ ___ ___!

Here is the last of my wishes.

Will you help me dry the ___ ___ ___ ___ ___ ___?

Everyday Words

Words to Learn

Write each word in the blank.

1. loud   _____

2. soft   _____

3. under   _____

4. over   _____

5. before   _____

6. after   _____

7. always   _____

8. never   _____

9. comes   _____

10. goes   _____

Write your hardest words again here:

_____

_____

_____

Match Up

When writing, some letters reach above the line and some go below it. Look at the shapes to help you find the right spelling word and write it in the matching shape.

under   after   goes   always   soft   before

1.
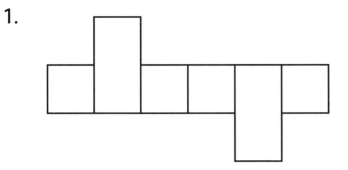

2.
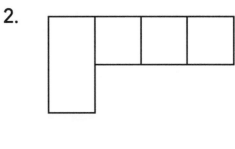

3.
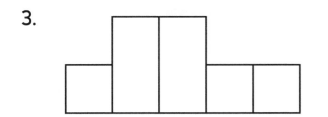

4.
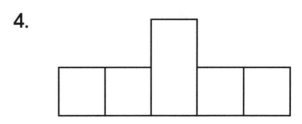

5.
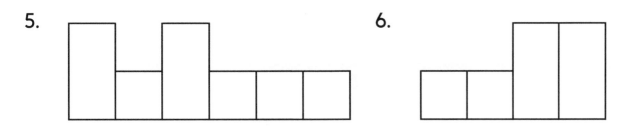

6.

Line Up!

Draw a line from each word in List A to the word that means the opposite in List B.
Write each word again in the line next to it.

List A

1. before _____

2. comes _____

3. loud _____

4. never _____

5. under _____

List B

soft _____

after _____

over _____

goes _____

always _____

Write a sentence using one of these words.

_____

_____

Merry-Go-Round

Start at any letter and move around the circle, either forward or backward, to find one of your spelling words. Circle the first letter. Write the word under each circle.

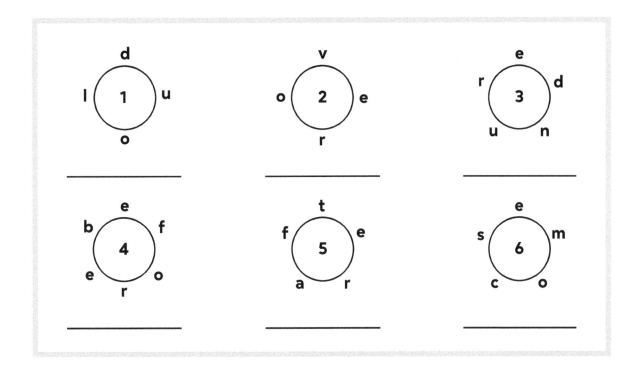

Box Stop

Write one word from the box in each blank. You will not use all the words.

always	under	comes	loud	before
never	over	goes	soft	after

1. My brother _____ to bed at nine o'clock.

2. I go to sleep _____ I read a story with my sister.

3. Sometimes our dog is so _____ that I wake up.

4. It is hard to train him to have a _____ bark!

5. I am happy in the morning. I am _____ glad to start a new day.

6. I don't like the day to end. I _____ want to go to bed!

Scramble

Write the correct spelling word for each set of scrambled letters.

1. s o g e ___ ___ ___ ___

2. v e r e n ___ ___ ___ ___ ___

3. f r e e o b ___ ___ ___ ___ ___ ___

4. t r e f a ___ ___ ___ ___ ___

5. t s f o ___ ___ ___ ___

6. a l y a w s ___ ___ ___ ___ ___ ___

7. d n e u r ___ ___ ___ ___ ___

8. o d u l ___ ___ ___ ___

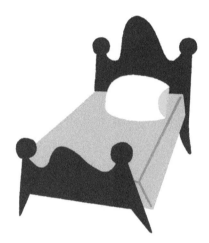

Write a sentence using one of these words.

_____

_____

If you need help with the spelling words,
look back at page 122.

Letter Sense

Add the missing letters to your spelling words so each sentence makes sense.

1. The rainy weather c ___ ___ ___ s and  ___ ___ s.

2. I have n___ ___ ___ ___ eaten kale, but I a___ ___ ___ ___ ___ like to try new foods.

3. We played a game b___ ___ ___ ___ ___ dinner and we watched TV ___ ___ t ___ ___ we ate.

4. Dad likes ___ ___ ___d music, but Mom likes ___ ___ f ___ music.

5. The gray cat hides u ___ ___ ___ ___ the sofa, but the brown cat runs ___ ___ ___ r the chair.

If you need help with the spelling words, look back at page 122.

Words to Learn

Write each word in the blank.

1. very _____

2. every _____

3. sight _____

4. right _____

5. said _____

6. says _____

7. because _____

8. around _____

9. could _____

10. again _____

Write your hardest words again here:

_____

_____

_____

Letter Slides

Slide letters from the first word down to the second using the arrow. Keep going, sliding letters from each word down to the word below it, until you have reached the end of each slide.

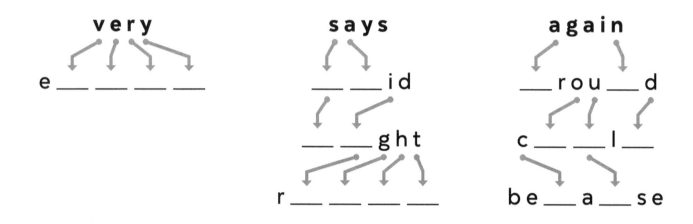

very

e __ __ __ __

says

__ __ i d

__ __ g h t

r __ __ __ __

again

__ r o u __ d

c __ __ l __

b e __ a __ s e

Write a sentence using one of these words.

_____

_____

130

Be Choosy!

Choose the best answer and circle it. Write the word in the blank.

1. I go to the zoo _____ summer with my grandpa.

   very   every   right

2. It is a great day _____ my grandpa is a lot of fun.

   because   around   says

3. "Maybe we can go two times this year," he _____.

   said   sight   could

4. I hope we can go _____ soon!

   right   very   again

5. We will walk all the way _____ the zoo.

   around   because   right

6. Then, we will have a snack and do it _____!

   sight   every   again

Tic-Tac-Toe

Circle every word spelled correctly. Draw a line across three of them to score a tic-tac-toe. Write the misspelled words correctly in the blanks.

becuase	around	cuold
agian	says	right
sigt	very	siad

_____

_____

_____

Follow the Clues

Write the spelling words that fit each clue. There will be several answers at first. You will write some spelling words more than once. For the last clue, there will be just one word. Which word will it be?

again	around	because	could	very
every	sight	right	said	says

1. Five words spelled with five letters

   _____   _____   _____

   _____   _____

2. Two words spelled with five letters and that rhyme with each other

   _____   _____

3. One word, spelled with five letters, that rhymes with another word on the list and is the opposite of left   _____

Word Search

Circle each word you find in the word search. Words may go up, down, across, or diagonally, both backward and forward. Write each word as you find it.

b	b	r	i	g	h	t	d
a	j	e	d	f	h	h	y
v	r	c	c	n	a	g	r
e	s	o	s	a	b	i	e
r	a	u	u	a	u	s	v
y	i	l	z	n	y	s	e
u	d	d	r	w	d	s	e
n	i	a	g	a	w	x	z

because _____

again _____

around _____

could _____

right _____

sight _____

said _____

says _____

every _____

very _____

Finish the Poem

Finish this rhyming poem. Use one of the spelling words from the box in each blank. If time allows, draw a picture to go with your poem on another piece of paper.

around	Could	again	said	sight	right

Our brown cat was white!

What a ___ ___ ___ ___ ___!

Is she all ___ ___ ___ ___? 18

We looked all ___ ___ ___ ___ ___ ___

Until we found

A pail of white paint!

___ ___ ___ ___ ___ we wash our cat?

Would she go along with that?

We tried again and ___ ___ ___ ___ ___ and yet . . .

Dad ___ ___ ___ ___ we should call the vet!

Fun Words

Words to Learn

Write each word in the blank.

1. trick   _____

2. treat   _____

3. movie   _____

4. popcorn   _____

5. airplane   _____

6. blimp   _____

7. train   _____

8. dream   _____

9. blink   _____

10. giggle   _____

Write your hardest words again here:

_____

_____

_____

Match Up

When writing, some letters reach above the line and some go below it. Look at the shapes to help you find the right spelling word and write it in the matching shape.

| treat | giggle | blimp | movie | train | blink |

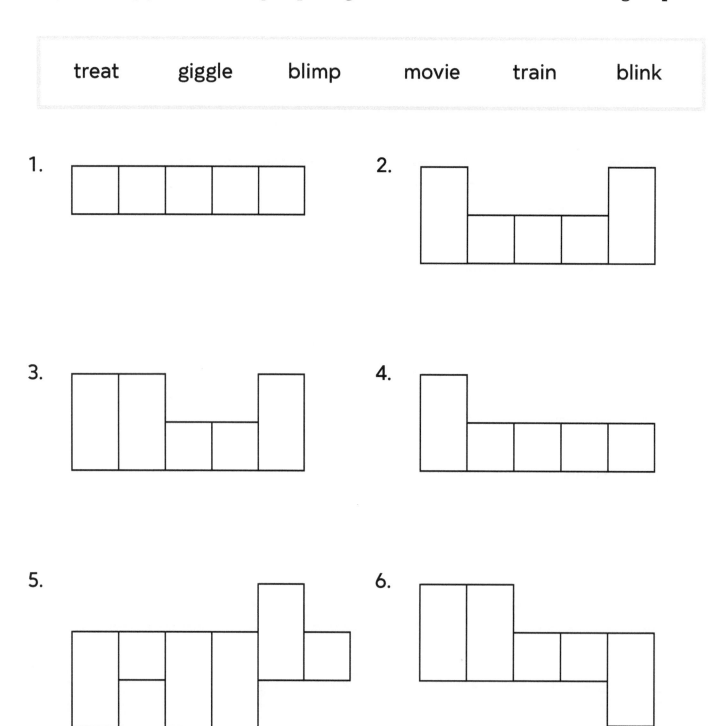

1.

2.

3.

4.

5.

6.

Box Stop

Write your words from the box in each blank. You will not use all the words.

trick	movie	airplane	train	blink
blimp	popcorn	treat	dream	giggle

1. What two things could you see in the sky?

   _____   _____

2. What would you do if you saw something funny? _____

3. What can you do in your sleep? _____

4. Find three words that begin with the same two consonants.

   _____   _____   _____

5. Write one sentence that uses movie and popcorn.

   _____

   _____

Merry-Go-Round

Start at any letter and move around the circle, either forward or backward, to find one of your spelling words. Circle the first letter. Write the word under each circle.

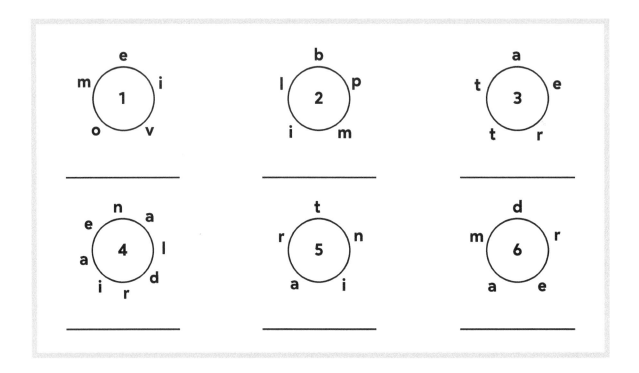

1. e · i · v · o · m

2. b · p · m · i · l

3. a · e · r · t · t

4. n · a · l · d · r · i · a · e

5. t · n · i · a · r

6. d · r · e · m · a · e

_____   _____   _____

_____   _____   _____

Letter Sense

Add the missing letters to your spelling words so each sentence makes sense.

1. Something fell from the sky, faster than I could b ___ ___ ___ ___

   my eyes.

2. It was not a plane, a bird, or even Superman. It was a

   ___ ___ ___ ___ p!

3. My dad frowned, but all my sister could do was g ___ ___ ___ I ___.

4. We flew on an a ___ ___ ___ ___ ___ n ___ to go visit my aunt.

5. I'm so glad you liked the magic show. What was your favorite

   ___ ___ ___ ___ k?

6. I thought I was late to school, but then I woke up. It was just a

   ___ ___ ___ ___ ___ !

If you need help with the spelling words,
look back at page 137.

Places, Please

Add each of your spelling words to this puzzle. Use the letters shown to help you. Cross off each word after you put it in the puzzle. Write your word again in the blank.

trick _____

treat _____

movie _____

popcorn _____

airplane _____

blimp _____

train _____

dream _____

blink _____

giggle _____

Scrambles

Write the correct spelling word for each set of scrambled letters.

1. o c n p p o r   __ __ __ __ __ __ __

2. m a r e d   __ __ __ __ __

3. l m b i p   __ __ __ __ __

4. e v o i m   __ __ __ __ __
   19

5. r e n i l a p a   __ __ __ __ __ __ __ __

6. i t a n r   __ __ __ __ __

7. r e a t t   __ __ __ __ __

8. c r t k i   __ __ __ __ __

Write a sentence using one of these words.

_____

_____

If you need help with the spelling words,
look back at page 137.

Words to Learn

Write each word in the blank.

1. ocean _____

2. beach _____

3. sailboat _____

4. surfing _____

5. swim _____

6. whistle _____

7. summer _____

8. winter _____

9. snowman _____

10. skate _____

Write your hardest words again here:

_____

_____

_____

Word Search

Circle each word you find in the word search. Words may go up, down, across, or diagonally, both backward and forward. Write each word as you find it.

s	c	b	e	a	c	h	g	m	q
u	e	l	t	s	i	h	w	i	y
r	t	s	u	m	m	e	r	w	t
f	t	a	o	b	l	i	a	s	x
i	p	y	k	y	j	l	x	g	g
n	q	r	u	d	t	v	p	s	f
g	u	w	i	n	t	e	r	g	q
y	o	d	o	c	e	a	n	k	m
v	n	a	m	w	o	n	s	r	c
h	n	o	p	s	k	a	t	e	x

ocean _____

beach _____

sailboat _____

surfing _____

summer _____

swim _____

whistle _____

winter _____

snowman _____

skate _____

Box Stop

Write your words from the box in each blank. You will not use all the words.

beach	surfing	swim	ocean	skate
summer	sailboat	whistle	winter	snowman

1. What two seasons are in the box?

   _____   _____

2. What are four things you might do or see at the ocean?

   _____   _____

   _____   _____

3. If you were to put all the words in the box in ABC order, which word would come first? _____

4. Circle any of these that you can do or would like to do:

   swim   whistle   skate

5. Write a sentence about a snowman.

   _____

   _____

Tic-Tac-Toe

Circle every word spelled correctly. Draw a line across three of them to score a tic-tac-toe. Write the misspelled words correctly in the blanks.

sumer	surffing	whisle
ocaen	sailboat	scate
winter	snowman	swim

_____

_____

_____

Crack the Code

Use the code to find your spelling words. Write each letter as you solve it.

1. % 1 + 3 2

   — — — — —
   s k a t e

2. ≈ ✱ ♦ 3 2 $

   — — — — — —
   w i n t e r

3. 5 4 2 + ♦

   — — — — —
   o c e a n

4. ≈ ‡ ✱ % 3 7 2

   — — — — — — —
   w h i s t l e

5. ✔ 2 + 4 ‡

   — — — — —
   b e a c h

6. % ♦ 5 ≈ 6 + ♦

   — — — — — — —
   s n o w m a n

1 = k	$ = r
2 = e	≈ = w
3 = t	% = s
4 = c	‡ = h
5 = o	+ = a
6 = m	♦ = n
7 = l	✔ = b
	✱ = i

Be Choosy!

Choose the best answer and circle it. Write the word in the blank.

1. Our family likes to go to the _____.

    summer   ocean   skate

2. If the waves are high enough, we can go _____.

    surfing   sailboat   swim

3. We like to take picnic food and eat on the _____.

    ocean   beach   summer

4. When it's time to leave, Dad gives a loud _____.

    skate   winter   whistle

5. The best thing to do in the winter is to build a _____.

    beach   whistle   snowman

Finish the Poem

Finish each little rhyming poem. Use one of the spelling words from the box in each blank.

winter	summer	skate	swim	beach	ocean

1. Let's race to reach the sandy ___ ___ ___ ___ ___.

2. Please close the gate when you go out to ___ ___ ___ ___ ___.

3. Before the light is dim we want to wade and ___ ___ ___ ___.

4. My mom says it's a bummer we've reached the end

   of ___ ___ ___ ___ ___ ___.
   ₂₀

5. Wear the sunscreen lotion if you are going to

   the ___ ___ ___ ___ ___.

6. I found a paper in my printer that tells me all about

   ___ ___ ___ ___ ___ ___.

Putting It All Together

In this last chapter, you'll solve 10 big puzzles. You will see many of the spelling words you learned in this book. Plus, you will find the last two secret letters to help you solve "The Case of the Hidden Gold"!

Letter Sense: Double Consonants

Add the correct set of double letters to your spelling words so each sentence makes sense.

1. The clown's hat was very fu ___ ___ y.

2. When we saw the hat, it was hard for us not to gi ___ ___ le !

3. The clown gave a boy a ba ___ ___ oon.

4. The boy was very ha ___ ___ y!

5. Have you ever petted a ra___ ___it ?

6. Have you held a new ki ___ ___ en?

7. I am sorry I did not see you last su ___ ___ er.

8. I am glad we are in the same cla ___ ◯.
   21

9. We can help each other learn to spe ___ ___ new words.

10. Do you know how to a ___ ___ big numbers?

11. My dad's bu ___ ___ y likes to come to our house.

12. He helps my dad cut the gra ___ ___.

13. He never gets cro ___ ___ with me.

14. My dad looks si ___ ___ y when he wears his big red nose.

15. Sometimes he wears big ye ___ ___ ow ears, too!

Line Up! Compound Words

We make compound words when we put two words together to form a new word with a new meaning. Some examples are *baseball* and *anyone*.

   You learned many compound words in this book. Do you know them all? In each set of words, draw a line from a word in column A to a word in column B to make a compound word. You might use a word more than once. Then, write all the words you make in the lines in column C.

A	B	C
1. pop	day	_____
2. birth	pack	_____
3. in	ground	_____
4. back	box	_____
5. sand	man	_____
6. snow	corn	_____
7. play	room	_____
8. lunch	side	_____
9. air	tub	_____
10. mail	fly	_____
11. bath	bug	_____
12. butter	boat	_____
13. sail	shine	_____
14. lady	plane	_____
15. sun	box	_____

Now write a sentence using your favorite compound word.

_____

_____

Places, Please: Long Vowel Sounds

You learned many words with long vowel sounds. Some of these words follow the vowel-consonant-silent e pattern, as in *side* and *lake*.

Finish spelling each word you learned by adding the missing vowel and the silent e at the end. Then, place each finished word into the puzzle. (The letters already in the puzzle may help you.)

1. j ___ k ___

2. s ___ f ___

3. w h ___ l ___

4. s n ___ k ___

5. w h ___ t ___

6. f ___ v ___

7. g r ___ d ___

8. s t ___ v ___

9. s l ___ d ___

10. n ___ n ___

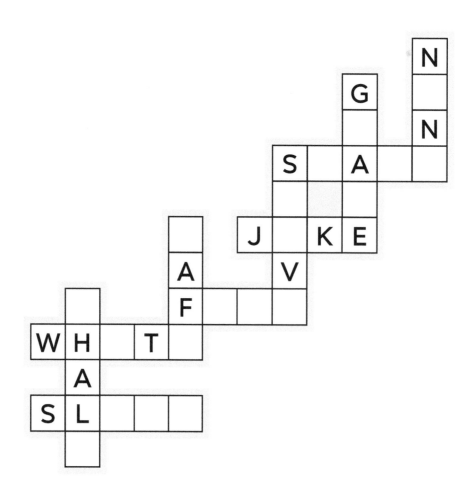

PUZZLE 124

Scrambles: Short and Long Vowels

Unscramble these words that have just one vowel. Write S in the box after the word if the vowel has a short sound (as in cat). Write L in the box after the word if the vowel has a long sound (as in both).

1. d s a _____ ☐   2. h t a p _____ ☐

3. m i s w _____ ☐   4. l i c d h _____ ☐

5. o g d _____ ☐   6. s f i h _____ ☐

7. k n i s _____ ☐   8. m l a p _____ ☐

9. x i s _____ ☐   10. n p o d _____ ☐

11. l g d o _____ ☐   12. u p j m _____ ☐

13. c u k d _____ ☐   14. e k s d _____ ☐

Write a sentence that uses one of the S words.

_____

_____

Write a sentence that uses one of the L words.

_____

_____

155

Be Choosy! Consonant Blends

Many spelling words begin with consonant blends. Choose the best consonant blend for each sentence. Circle the blend and write the whole word in the blank.

1. It will be fun to ride a ___ ___ ain to New York. _____

    sh   tr   fr

2. A ___ ___ ail carries a shell on its back. _____

    sn   ch   sh

3. I want to learn to ice ___ ___ ate. _____

    gr   tr   sk

4. Let's ___ ___ udy our math facts. _____

    st   cl   sh

5. My ___ ___ andma made this shirt for me. _____

    br   gr   fr

6. When the lights went out, the room was ___ ___ ack. _____

   gr   st   bl

7. My ___ ___ other was very happy on his birthday. _____

   cl   br   tr

8. I know how to ___ ___ aw a duck. _____

   sh   pr   dr

9. I am very ___ ___ oud of my little sister. _____

   pr   fl   ch

10. Will you be my ___ ___ iend? _____

   br   bl   fr

Crossword: Silent Letters

First, add the missing silent letter to each word in the list. Then, use one of these words for each clue in the crossword.

hom ___   clim ___

lis ___ en   lov ___

cou ___ d   whis ___ le

___ rite   hors ___

wa ___ k   ta ___ k

Down

1. My aunt lets me ride her black _____.

2. It's nice to spend a day at _____.

3. I want to _____ this tall tree.

5. I will _____ a letter to my uncle.

6. Please _____ carefully to what I am saying.

7. Let's _____ to the park.

Across

4. _____ you please help me?

5. My grandpa has a loud _____!

8. Don't _____ too loudly in the library.

9. I _____ my mother.

Super Tic-Tac-Toe: Vowel Teams

Some spelling words have tricky vowel teams. Circle all the words spelled correctly on this big tic-tac-toe game. Then, draw a line to connect FOUR words in a row. Write the other words correctly in the lines below.

blue	gruop	ocean	aroond
cuoch	eihgt	four	house
gaot	luagh	beach	dreem
because	agian	mean	read

_____

_____

_____

_____

Merry-Go-Rounds
TWO-SYLLABLE WORDS

You learned many words with two syllables. Can you find 12 of them on these merry-go-rounds?

Start at any letter and move around the circle, either forward or backward, to find one of your spelling words. Circle the first letter. Write the word under each circle.

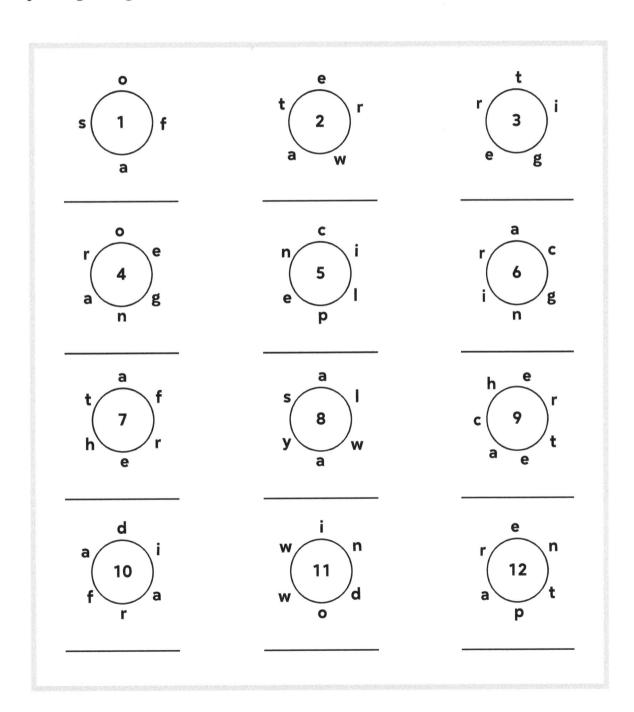

Word Search: Misspellings

Look at each of these spelling words. If the word is spelled correctly, circle it in the list and circle it in the word search puzzle. Words may go up, down, across, or diagonally, both forward and backward.

   If the word is not spelled right, cross it out and write it correctly in the blanks at the right. (Hint: There are 12 spelling words in the puzzle.)

l	t	f	o	s	z	m	j	t
k	q	s	t	l	e	p	e	e
r	y	n	e	y	l	a	l	p
e	u	m	c	t	e	p	p	r
a	a	w	a	y	v	e	r	a
c	m	o	t	h	e	r	u	c
x	m	n	m	u	n	l	p	o
y	n	o	n	w	n	e	w	m
h	n	e	v	e	s	a	f	b
c	z	m	q	i	g	r	u	m
r	o	o	l	f	e	n	k	f

1. movie
2. befor
3. purple
4. eleven
5. carpet
6. evry
7. camel
8. siad
9. paper
10 togeter
11. learn
12. aunt
13. twelf
14. luod
15. soft
16. floor
17. zeroe
18. mother
19. seven
20. angery

Write misspelled words correctly here:

_____

_____

_____

_____

_____

_____

_____

Hidden Message: Word Endings

For each clue, choose a word from the box plus a word ending. Write the complete word in the white squares in the puzzle. You will spell an answer to the riddle, *What should you do when you find an elephant asleep in your bed?*

Words:

chair	pet
gloom	tree
joy	flower
bore	help
toy	camp
game	thank
kite	scare
hope	bird
dish	

Endings:

-s or –es

-ing

-ful

-y

-ed or –d

1. Animal friends
2. Feeling down or blue
3. Full of fear
4. Large plants with trunks
5. Staying outside in tents
6. Places to sit
7. Full of joy
8. Things you can play
9. Fly these in the sky with string on a windy day
10. Blooms
11. Full of thanks
12. How you feel when there is nothing to do
13. Animals that fly
14. Full of hope
15. Plates, cups, and bowls
16. Gives help
17. Blocks, cars, dolls, games, and more

1												
2												
3												
4												
5												
6												
7												
8												
9												
10												
11												
12												
13												
14												
15												
16												
17												
						e						

What should you do when you find an elephant asleep in your bed?

__ __ __ __ __   __ __ __ __ __ __ __ __ __

__ __ __ e!

SOLVE THE MYSTERY

When we left Jane, Karl, Grandma, and her dog, Franklin, they were trying to find something. What was it?

That's right! They were trying to find gold coins. Grandma had found an old note from her grandfather that said he had hidden three gold coins he wanted her to find.

Karl, Jane, and Grandma looked by the apple trees. They looked by the pond. But they did not see the gold.

Now you can tell them where to find the gold. With Franklin's help, you have been working hard in this spelling book. You have solved puzzles and you have found the special letters under the magnifying glasses.

Let's read the question once more, then fill in the answer!

Where are the gold coins hidden?

They are __ __ __ __ __   __ __ __ __ __ __ __ __'__

 1   2   3   4   5   6   7   8   9 10 11 12 13 14

__ __ __ __ __ __ __ __!

15 16 17 18 19 20 21 22

Now turn the page to check your answer.

The answer is . . .

UNDER FRANKLIN'S DOGHOUSE!

Here is your Word Detective badge. **Well done! You have earned it.**

DON'T FORGET:
You can get 20 free bonus puzzles at
CallistoMediaBooks.com/WordDetective2

ANSWER KEY

PUZZLE 1

1. baby
2. aunt
3. sister
4. family
5. uncle
6. brother

PUZZLE 2

1. uncle, aunt
2. mother, brother, father, sister
3. baby, family, home, pets

PUZZLE 3

1. father
2. mother
3. uncle
4. aunt
5. sister
6. brother
7. home
8. pets

PUZZLE 4

PUZZLE 5

1. aunt
2. mother
3. family
4. uncle
5. home
6. sister

PUZZLE 6

1. uncle
2. baby
3. father
4. pets
5. sister

PUZZLE 7

Corrections: grandpa, caring, together, sharing

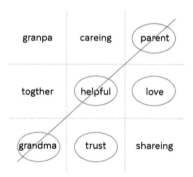

PUZZLE 8

PUZZLE 9

1. together
2. parent
3. grandma
4. love
5. sharing

PUZZLE 10

grandpa, grandma, child, love caring, sharing, parent, helpful trust, together

PUZZLE 11

1. trust
2. sharing
3. love
4. grandpa
5. parent
6. grandma

PUZZLE 12

1. home
2. trust
3. sharing
4. child
5. parent
6. caring
7. helpful
8. together

PUZZLE 13

1. grin
2. team
3. group
4. funny
5. games
6. outside

PUZZLE 14

1. grin
2. group
3. toys
4. funny
5. games
6. outside
7. buddy
8. inside

PUZZLE 15

1. pal, buddy
2. group, team
3. inside, outside
4. toys, games

PUZZLE 16

PUZZLE 17

Corrections: buddy, toys, group, funny, outside

buddie	gruop	(games)
(team)	(grin)	(inside)
toyes	funy	otside

PUZZLE 18

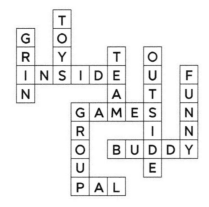

PUZZLE 19

1. laugh
2. give
3. talk
4. listen
5. party
6. joke

PUZZLE 20

1. talk
2. joke
3. friend
4. party
5. laugh
6. listen
7. children
8. balloon

PUZZLE 21

1. birthday
2. children
3. joke
4. give
5. balloon

PUZZLE 22

1. balloon
2. friend
3. birthday
4. listen
5. children
6. laugh

PUZZLE 23

1. friend
2. laugh, joke
3. listen
4. party, birthday
5. talk

PUZZLE 24

1. party
2. laugh
3. give
4. birthday
5. friend
6. listen
7. talk
8. children

PUZZLE 25

1. learn
2. think
3. paint
4. spell
5. count
6. write

PUZZLE 26

spell, learn, read
work, write, draw, add
paint, think, count

PUZZLE 27

Corrections: spell, learn, count, draw, work

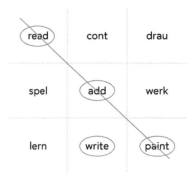

171

PUZZLE 28

1. read
2. learn
3. count
4. add
5. work

PUZZLE 29

1. think
2. draw
3. count
4. work
5. learn
6. write

PUZZLE 30

PUZZLE 31

1. pencil
2. teacher
3. shelf
4. study
5. paper
6. desk
7. backpack
8. lunchroom

PUZZLE 32

1. grade
2. class
3. shelf
4. teacher
5. pencil
6. study

PUZZLE 33

1. class or grade
2. shelf, desk, backpack
3. teacher
4. lunchroom
5. study
6. pencil

PUZZLE 34

s	q	z	l	i	c	n	e	p
h	s	s	b	k	j	v	z	j
e	t	y	a	e	d	a	r	g
l	u	n	c	h	r	o	o	m
f	d	w	k	w	v	a	l	c
n	y	d	p	g	z	a	w	l
a	i	p	a	p	e	r	j	a
r	e	h	c	a	e	t	q	s
p	y	e	k	s	e	d	g	s

PUZZLE 35

1. pencil
2. shelf
3. grade
4. desk
5. teacher
6. paper
7. backpack
8. class

PUZZLE 36

(Answers may vary slightly.)
1. backpack, paper, grade, pencil, teacher, shelf
2. backpack, paper, pencil
3. paper, pencil
4. paper

PUZZLE 37

dog, frog, goat
rabbit, kitten, chicken, duck
fish, sheep, horse

PUZZLE 38

1. horse
2. sheep
3. kitten
4. frog
5. rabbit
6. duck

PUZZLE 39

1. chicken
2. dog
3. sheep
4. kitten
5. duck

PUZZLE 40

Corrections: kitten, chicken, rabbit, goat, sheep

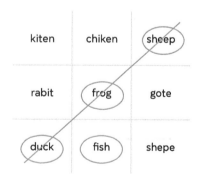

PUZZLE 41

1. dog, kitten, rabbit, sheep, goat, horse
2. kitten, rabbit
3. rabbit

PUZZLE 42

1. horse
2. chicken
3. duck
4. fish
5. frog
6. dog
7. kitten
8. sheep

PUZZLE 43

1. lion
2. snail
3. shark
4. camel
5. ladybug
6. whale

PUZZLE 44

1. camel
2. tiger
3. goose
4. snake
5. ladybug
6. whale
7. shark
8. butterfly

PUZZLE 45

1. whale, snail
2. shark, snake
3. goose, ladybug, butterfly
4. whale, shark
5. Answers will vary.

PUZZLE 46

1. whale
2. camel
3. lion
4. goose
5. tiger
6. snake

PUZZLE 47

PUZZLE 48

1. snail
2. goose
3. whale
4. snake
5. tiger
6. shark

PUZZLE 49

walk, water, trees, grass, air
climb, jump, skip
pond, pool

PUZZLE 50

1. water
2. climb
3. pool
4. walk
5. skip

PUZZLE 51

1. walk, jump, skip, climb
2. Answers will vary.
3. pond, pool
4. trees, grass
5. Answers will vary.

PUZZLE 52

Corrections: climb, skip, walk, pool, grass

clim	scip	water
trees	air	jump
wak	pol	gras

PUZZLE 53

1. walk
2. grass
3. jump
4. water
5. pool
6. pond
7. climb
8. skip

PUZZLE 54

1. air
2. trees
3. jump
4. pond
5. grass
6. Water

173

PUZZLE 55

1. kites
2. slide
3. camping
4. sandbox
5. sunshine
6. flowers

PUZZLE 56

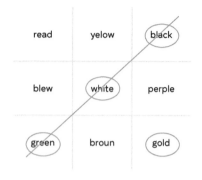

PUZZLE 57

1. playground
2. wind
3. path
4. sandbox
5. flowers

PUZZLE 58

1. birds
2. wind
3. slide
4. flowers
5. kites
6. sandbox

PUZZLE 59

1. kites, flowers, birds
2. kites, birds
3. birds
4. Answers will vary.

PUZZLE 60

1. camping
2. sunshine
3. playground
4. slide
5. sandbox
6. wind, kites

PUZZLE 61

1. brown
2. orange
3. green
4. purple
5. white
6. black

PUZZLE 62

1. red
2. yellow
3. gold
4. blue
5. purple
6. white
7. orange
8. black

PUZZLE 63

1. gold
2. black
3. yellow, orange
4. white
5. blue
6. brown
7. purple

PUZZLE 64

Corrections: red, yellow, blue, purple, brown

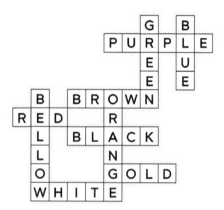

PUZZLE 65

1. blue
2. green
3. gold
4. brown
5. orange
6. purple
7. yellow
8. white

PUZZLE 66

PUZZLE 67

1. four
2. seven
3. eight
4. eleven
5. zero
6. seven

PUZZLE 68

PUZZLE 69

1. zero
2. four
3. nine
4. seven
5. twelve
6. eight

PUZZLE 70

four, zero

nine, ten, seven, eleven

six, five, eight, twelve

PUZZLE 71

1. five, seven, nine, eleven
2. seven, eleven
3. eleven

PUZZLE 72

0	zero
1	one
2	two
3	three
4	four
5	five
6	six
7	seven
8	eight
9	nine
10	ten
11	eleven
12	twelve
13	thirteen
14	fourteen

PUZZLE 73

1. glad
2. silly
3. scared
4. lost
5. strong
6. angry

PUZZLE 74

1. glad, sad
2. glad
3. angry
4. silly
5. scared
6. Answers will vary.

PUZZLE 75

1. safe
2. silly
3. scared
4. lost
5. strong
6. angry

PUZZLE 76

1. happy
2. lost
3. glad
4. angry
5. silly
6. sad
7. scared
8. strong

PUZZLE 77

1. glad
2. sad
3. safe
4. lost
5. mean
6. scared

PUZZLE 78

```
S C A R E D
A         |
F     A
M E A N     H
      G L A D
      R   P
S I L L Y   P
T   O       Y
R   S A D
O   T
N
G
```

PUZZLE 79

1. gloomy, joyful, hopeful, thankful
2. sorry, cross, bored
3. hurt, proud, afraid

PUZZLE 80

1. proud
2. bored
3. hopeful
4. afraid
5. cross
6. thankful

PUZZLE 81

Corrections: bored, afraid, gloomy, hurt, hopeful

bord	afriad	(thankful)
glomy	hert	(proud)
(sorry)	hopful	(joyful)

PUZZLE 82

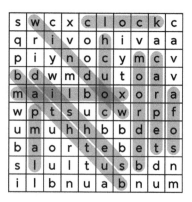

PUZZLE 83

1. joyful
2. sorry, hurt
3. gloomy
4. bored
5. hopeful
6. proud

PUZZLE 84

1. proud
2. bored
3. afraid
4. scared
5. joyful
6. sorry

PUZZLE 85

1. roof
2. stove
3. house
4. floor
5. door
6. table

PUZZLE 86

1. room, broom
2. house
3. floor, door
4. sink
5. roof
6. Answers will vary.

PUZZLE 87

1. roof
2. sink
3. floor
4. chairs
5. house
6. stove

PUZZLE 88

1. floor
2. broom
3. sink
4. stove
5. door
6. house
7. chairs
8. table

PUZZLE 89

PUZZLE 90

house, door, floor, broom, room, table

PUZZLE 91

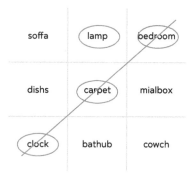

PUZZLE 92

1. bathtub
2. dishes
3. clock
4. mailbox
5. window

PUZZLE 93

Corrections: sofa, dishes, mailbox, bathtub, couch

soffa	lamp	bedroom
dishs	carpet	mialbox
clock	bathub	cowch

PUZZLE 94

1. sofa
2. couch
3. carpet
4. bedroom
5. bathtub
6. clock

PUZZLE 95

1. dishes
2. bathtub
3. couch
4. window
5. carpet
6. bedroom

PUZZLE 96

clock, bathtub, bedroom, mailbox, dishes

PUZZLE 97

1. always
2. goes
3. after
4. under
5. before
6. soft

PUZZLE 98

1. before-after
2. comes-goes
3. loud-soft
4. never-always
5. under-over

PUZZLE 99

1. loud
2. over
3. under
4. before
5. after
6. comes

PUZZLE 100

1. goes
2. after
3. loud
4. soft
5. always
6. never

PUZZLE 101

1. goes
2. never
3. before
4. after
5. soft
6. always
7. under
8. loud

PUZZLE 102

1. comes, goes
2. never, always
3. before, after
4. loud, soft
5. under, over

PUZZLE 103

very, every
says, said, sight, right
again, around, could, because

PUZZLE 104

1. every
2. because
3. said
4. again
5. around
6. again

PUZZLE 105

Corrections: because, could, again, sight, said

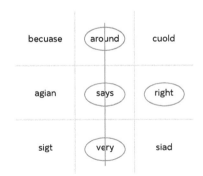

PUZZLE 106

1. again, could, every, sight, right
2. sight, right
3. right

PUZZLE 107

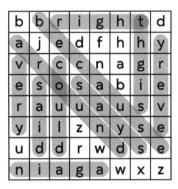

PUZZLE 108

sight, right, around, Could, again, said

PUZZLE 109

1. movie
2. treat
3. blink
4. train
5. giggle
6. blimp

PUZZLE 110

1. airplane, blimp
2. giggle
3. dream
4. trick, train, treat
5. Answers will vary.

PUZZLE 111

1. movie
2. blimp
3. treat
4. airplane
5. train
6. dream

PUZZLE 112

1. blink
2. blimp
3. giggle
4. airplane
5. trick
6. dream

PUZZLE 113

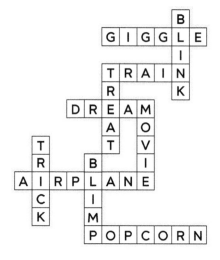

PUZZLE 114

1. popcorn
2. dream
3. blimp
4. movie
5. airplane
6. train
7. treat
8. trick

PUZZLE 115

s	c	b	e	a	c	h	g	m	q
u	e	l	t	s	i	h	w	i	y
r	t	s	u	m	m	e	r	w	t
f	t	a	o	b	l	i	a	s	x
i	p	y	k	y	j	l	x	g	g
n	q	r	u	d	t	v	p	s	f
g	u	w	i	n	t	e	r	g	q
y	o	d	o	c	e	a	n	k	m
v	n	a	m	w	o	n	s	r	c
h	n	o	p	s	k	a	t	e	x

PUZZLE 116

1. summer, winter
2. beach, surfing, ocean, sailboat
3. beach
4. Answers will vary.
5. Answers will vary.

PUZZLE 117

Corrections: summer, surfing, whistle, ocean, skate

PUZZLE 118

1. skate
2. winter
3. ocean
4. whistle
5. beach
6. snowman

PUZZLE 119

1. ocean
2. surfing
3. beach
4. whistle
5. snowman

PUZZLE 120

1. beach
2. skate
3. swim
4. summer
5. ocean
6. winter

PUZZLE 121

1. funny
2. giggle
3. balloon
4. happy
5. rabbit
6. kitten
7. summer
8. class
9. spell
10. add
11. buddy
12. grass
13. cross
14. silly
15. yellow

PUZZLE 122

Compound words (in any order):
1. popcorn
2. birthday
3. inside
4. backpack
5. sandbox
6. snowman
7. playground
8. lunchroom
9. airplane
10. mailbox
11. bathtub
12. butterfly
13. sailboat
14. ladybug
15. sunshine

PUZZLE 123

1. joke
2. safe
3. whale
4. snake
5. white
6. five
7. grade
8. stove
9. slide
10. nine

Sentences will vary.

PUZZLE 124

(Some have more than one possible answer. This book's spelling words are shown here.)

1. sad   S
2. path   S
3. swim   S
4. child   L
5. dog   S
6. fish   S
7. sink   S
8. lamp   S
9. six   S
10. pond   S
11. gold   L
12. jump   S
13. duck   S
14. desk   S

Sentences will vary.

PUZZLE 125

1. tr, train
2. sn, snail
3. sk, skate
4. st, study
5. gr, grandma
6. bl, black
7. br, brother
8. dr, draw
9. pr, proud
10. fr, friend

PUZZLE 126

PUZZLE 127

Corrections: group, around, couch, eight, goat, laugh, dream, again

blue	gruop	(ocean)	aroond
cuoch	eihgt	(four)	(house)
gaot	luagh	(beach)	dreem
(because)	agian	(mean)	(read)

PUZZLE 128

1. sofa
2. water
3. tiger
4. orange
5. pencil
6. caring
7. father
8. always
9. teacher
10. afraid
11. window
12. parent

PUZZLE 129

Correct words to find in the puzzle: movie, purple, eleven, carpet, camel, paper, learn, aunt, soft, floor, mother, seven.

Corrected words: before, every, said, together, twelve, loud, zero, angry

l	t	f	o	s	z	m	j	t
k	q	s	t	l	e	p	e	e
r	y	n	e	y	l	a	l	p
e	u	m	c	t	e	p	p	r
a	a	w	a	y	v	e	r	a
c	m	o	t	h	e	r	u	c
x	m	n	m	u	n	l	p	o
y	n	o	n	w	n	e	w	m
h	n	e	v	e	s	a	f	b
c	z	m	q	i	g	r	u	m
r	o	o	l	f	e	n	k	f

PUZZLE 130

#	1	2	3	4	5	6	7	8	9	10	11	12
1			p	e	t	s						
2					g	l	o	o	m	y		
3		s	c	a	r	e	d					
4			t	r	e	e	s					
5			c	a	m	p	i	n	g			
6	c	h	a	i	r	s						
7					j	o	y	f	u	l		
8				g	a	m	e	s				
9			k	i	t	e	s					
10			f	l	o	w	e	r	s			
11					t	h	a	n	k	f	u	l
12			b	o	r	e	d					
13				b	i	r	d	s				
14			h	o	p	e	f	u	l			
15		d	i	s	h	e	s					
16				h	e	l	p	f	u	l		
17			t	o	y	s						
						e						

SLEEP SOMEWHERE ELSE!

ACKNOWLEDGMENTS

I would like to thank:

EclipseCrossword puzzle engine ©Green Eclipse, available for free use at www. eclipsecrossword.com

Word Search Creator V1.0 © Matthew Wellings

Dictionaries that gave me ideas for some of my puzzles, in particular two longtime favorites from my personal bookshelf:

Abate, Frank, ed. *Oxford Desktop Dictionary and Thesaurus, American Edition.* (New York: Berkley Books, 1997.)

de Mello Vianna, Fernando, ed. *Children's Dictionary.* (Boston: Houghton Mifflin, 1979.)

My husband, Keith, who was always ready to wash dishes, fold laundry, and run errands to allow me more time to write. He's the best!

ABOUT THE AUTHOR

ANN RICHMOND FISHER is a former classroom teacher. She's also a wife and mother. She's known these days as "Granny Annie" to two beloved children whose middle names just happen to be Jane and Karl!

Ann has a degree in elementary education from Northern Michigan University. She and her husband, Keith, have lived in Michigan, Indiana, Ireland, and Pennsylvania. They now reside in Ohio.

After teaching in a classroom for six years, Ann chose to be a stay-at-home mom to her two children, Bryce and Betsy. Her love for teaching, learning, and words drew her to the world of freelance writing. She sold her first puzzles to *Highlights for Children* when her kids were preschoolers.

Now those "kids" are in their thirties and Ann is still writing. She's published more than 60 books, posters, and other products for a dozen publishers. She owns two websites: www.spelling-words-well.com and www.word-game-world.com.